Sincerely, Ty Cobb

Other books by Hank O'Neal

Sincerely, Ty Cobb

A Baseball Memoir

YOUNG, CLEVELAND

HANK O'NEAL

TCU Press

FORT WORTH, TEXAS

Library of Congress Cataloging-in-Publication Data

Names: O'Neal, Hank, author.
Title: Sincerely, Ty Cobb : a baseball memoir / Hank O'Neal.
Description: Fort Worth : TCU Press, [2020] | Summary: "Sincerely, Ty Cobb
　　　traces ten years of a child's life in baseball, from his first struggles
　　　on the sandlot to his final high school game. It is fully illustrated
　　　with period memorabilia, highlighted by twelve pages of handwritten
　　　letters from Ty Cobb, plus others from Hall of Fame players like Eddie
　　　Walsh and Frankie Frisch. The story is illustrated with old programs,
　　　tobacco and bubble gum cards, autographed photographs, including two
　　　from Cobb, plus others from Cy Young, Frankie Frisch, all the 1954
　　　Syracuse Chiefs, Rogers Hornsby, George Sisler and many, others"—
　　　Provided by publisher.
Identifiers: LCCN 2020001838 | ISBN 9780875657493 (paperback)
Subjects: LCSH: Cobb, Ty, 1886–1961—Correspondence. | O'Neal,
　　　Hank—Childhood and youth. | Baseball players—United States—Biography.
　　　| Baseball—Collectibles—United States. | LCGFT: Biographies. |
　　　Autobiographies. | Personal correspondence.
Classification: LCC GV865.A1 O64 2020 | DDC 796.357092/273—dc23
LC record available at https://lccn.loc.gov/2020001838

TCU Box 298300
Fort Worth, Texas 76129
817.257.7822
www.prs.tcu.edu
To order books: 1.800.826.8911

Design by Preston Thomas

FOR

Curtis Austin Christian (1884–1967) of Macon and Royston, Georgia, and Tyler, Texas, Ty Cobb's teammate in Royston, Georgia, around 1899–1900. The two men not only played together as teenagers, but both wound up in cemeteries called Rose Hill—one in Tyler, Texas; the other in Royston, Georgia, 790 miles apart.

CONTENTS

Doubleday

February 6, 1992

Mr. Hank O'Neal
830 Broadway
New York, NY 10003

Dear Hank

Thank you so much for sending me SINCERELY, TY COBB. It is absolutely enchanting, a touching story of the kindness of heroes and the innocence of little boys. Unfortunately, it does seem a little short for a book, and I really don't know what we would do with it at Doubleday. It was a pleasure to read, however, and I thank you for sharing it with me. I wish you all the best in finding it the perfect home.

best always

Jackie

Jacqueline Kennedy Onassis
Senior Editor

enc.

AUTHOR'S NOTE

I wrote the first version of *Sincerely, Ty Cobb* in 1991. I had once discussed my mother's 1930s teenage scrapbook with Jacqueline Onassis, who liked it but was unsure what to do with it, as was I. Many years later this scrapbook became a key element in *Preserving Lives* (TCU Press, 2018). Her initial interest in my mother's scrapbook led me to think she might also react positively to my draft of *Sincerely, Ty Cobb*, which I sent to her in early 1992. Jackie replied in February and after I'd received the world's most gracious rejection letter, we spoke and I suggested I could always make the book a bit longer. She said she'd be happy to have a look once I had done this.

It took me longer than I thought. I was deeply involved with the production of jazz, blues, and big band festivals at sea, jazz CDs for Chiaroscuro, and completing *Charlie Parker—The Funky Blues Date,* which would be published in 1995 by Filipacchi. By the time I finished the new version of *Sincerely, Ty Cobb* in late 1993 and Margaret Whitton had added her introduction, Jackie was ill. She died in May 1994. Much saddened, I put the book on the shelf, tinkered with it a bit in 2005, but did nothing with it until it occurred to me that it might be an ideal book to continue the story told in *Preserving Lives*.

FOREWORD

A baseball card or autograph collection is an iconography of the early psyche. It is a membership card in a nonexclusive club that bonds Americans across time, race, sense, and sex.

Maybe because I was in the last throes of adolescence, I wasn't ready for Hank's collection when we met.

Hank lived in an apartment above his Greenwich Village recording studio/loft. It served as a sort of salon for jazz musicians, photographers, painters, actors, and spies who breezed in and out at all hours in various states of consciousness and creativity. There was even a mysterious broken dancer or two recovering in the rooms upstairs. It was an odd bohemian finishing school for me. Hank would wander through in between making recordings of underappreciated or forgotten jazz artists on his Chiaroscuro label. Some of whom he would rehab and restore, an early impulse that prefigured his helping to create the Jazz Foundation of America. In between we would talk history, theater, art, politics, but never once about baseball. Years later, I stopped by another of Hank's beautiful loft spaces to pick up one of his photographs and mentioned, only slightly abashed, that I was on my way to a baseball card show to get a Lefty Groves autograph. "You like that stuff?" Hank's slow grin and blinking eyes were usually a preamble to a surprise. I should have known. Many artists are pack rats, and Hank, much to his wife's chagrin, is a champion. Still, that Saturday afternoon, even knowing Hank's acquisitive nature, I was unprepared for his baseball stash.

The first scrapbook was as eccentric and rangy as the adult Hank had become. I think he probably said something like "Golly, if you like this stuff, I have some others." Hank, for all his accomplishments, rarely takes himself seriously. He offhandedly dropped the Mantle ball, the Connie Mack ball, and another scrapbook in my greedy hands. Then he dropped the bombshell. He had had correspondence with Ty Cobb. He tossed the pages of another scrapbook back. I approached this scrapbook with as much reverence as if it contained the Dead Sea scrolls. Okay, maybe more.

Tyrus Raymond Cobb was exceedingly superstitious when on a hitting streak; he ate the same breakfast, took the same route to the ballpark, hung his towel on the same hook, and refused to clean his uniform. Habits that were not meant to endear him to his already antagonized teammates. In rural Georgia at the turn of the century, when your mother murders your father and gets acquitted, you too might draw the conclusion that the gods are to be appeased. Despite fatuous Hollywood "sexed up" conjecture, minimal research reveals that after a married life of abuse, the conclusion the jury drew was that abusive Papa Cobb probably got what was coming to him. Juries in Georgia, even today, would be unlikely to spare an adulteress. More interestingly but less graphic perhaps is the effect this had on young Tyrus.

Children who witness abuse are as affected as if it has happened to them. Or was he spared? He never met an insult real or imagined he let slide.

When he checked into the hospital, dying of cancer and complications, he carried a brown paper bag containing nearly $1 million in securities, a loaded German Luger, and a bottle of bourbon. Estimates of his estate ran between $6 to $11 million. He died at the age of seventy-four, estranged from most of his family, lonely, bitter, and resentful. Casey Stengel, a one-time opponent, for once at a loss for words, said of Cobb, "It was like he was super human."

Cobb was an anomaly in an era that liked its ballplayers brawny and dumb; Cobb, it was said, "out-thought the opposition." In his autobiography *My Life in Baseball*, as well as in the articles reprinted here and in his letters to young Hank, Cobb reveals an old-fashioned writing style reminiscent of Victorian sportswriters.

Although most of Cobb's previous records have been eclipsed, his lifetime batting average of .367 from the "dead ball" era seems destined to stand (despite chemical enhancements of modern-day players) for as long as baseball keeps records.

I think that Hank's collection was possibly built as a bulwark against the transience of his childhood: objects can speak to us and define a place of permanence inside our hearts. Many Americans have a "lost" baseball dream. Whatever happened to my Sadaharu Oh autographed ball? Is that what Jacques Barzun meant about getting to know Americans via their national pastime? In our yearning to be part of something we love and our eventual exclusion from it lies the common thread of the lost summers of childhood, when the realities of the world have yet to intrude upon us. Or, if the realities of the adult world have, as in Cobb's case, baseball provides a haven, a just structure, a respite from the baffling unfairness, a defined yet limitless field where you are judged by simpler standards. You throw the ball; you hit the ball and run. Deceptively simple, like life. And it prepares us for the difficult task of loving what excludes us and makes us grow up. Sort of.

As possessor of my own baseball heritage, I can converse with a wide range of other Americans, of any class, gender (well, some of the guys are a little nervous at first), region, or race. It becomes a visa to other conversations. It is the collective gum that moves us towards each other. But we only share those lost baseball stories, feeling a little shy at first, with those we sense harbor their own stories. What in young Hank's carefully polite letter made "Mr. Mean" of baseball respond? Was it the mention of Hank's grandfather? Was it Cobb trying to right the slurs of the sportswriters? What in Hank's longing letter to a hero, out of the hundreds he must have received, made Cobb, the most demonically driven competitor, respond?

Here is Hank's lost baseball story, and possibly a little of yours in some small way. To an America increasingly in transit, I'd say don't leave that bat behind. It is as emblematic as Rosebud or the yearnings for a game of catch in mid-winter. These lost totems of connection can return and catch the heart in unexpected ways. They can renew your eyes, or reconnect you with a former simpler self. Try mentioning it the next time you are talking fastball, curve, or slurve. Or that insane call by the umpire. Take the first step in revealing your lost baseball dream. My guess is you will be rewarded with your new friend's own version, and if you listen carefully you will find out much about what he or she is really made of. In Hank's case, you will be richly rewarded.

—Margaret Whitton

AUTHOR'S NOTE: Margaret Whitton was a noted actor and director, on Broadway and off, on the small TV screen and the big one in movie theaters. Her baseball credits include hundreds of games in the Broadway Show League that still fields teams regularly in New York City's Central Park; the role of the wicked owner of the Cleveland Indians, Rachel Phelps, in *Major League* and *Major League II*; as well as the inspiration for and cowriter of *Bull Durham*, no matter how the credits read. She also had four season tickets behind the Yankee's dugout at the real Yankee Stadium where I sometimes sat with her and her husband, Warren Spector. They were good seats; one day Jack Nicholson sat in front of me and we had an animated chat agreeing that the crowd was not being kind to Cecil Fielder.

Marg was also the last person with whom I tossed a real baseball, a long time ago, and she could throw it very well. I asked her to write this foreword in the early 1990s when I took Mrs. Onassis's advice and expanded my first draft of *Sincerely, Ty Cobb*. I met Marg much earlier, in 1968, when she was a budding, somewhat directionless but fiercely determined teenage actress. We were pals for nearly fifty years. She died in 2016, and I miss her deeply.

Sincerely, Ty Cobb

❧ A Dusty Sandlot ❧

I often wonder why I remember so much about playing baseball when I was a kid growing up in Fort Worth. I don't remember as much about fishing trips to Eagle Mountain Lake or movies at the Bowie, the closest movie theater a few blocks away on red-bricked Camp Bowie Boulevard, or looking for fossils at Possum Kingdom or even my classmates at Crestwood, my kindergarten through fourth-grade school. Why baseball? Maybe it has to do with remembering more about summer than winter; summer means sunny days, no school, bare feet, and baseball. Winter is about bad weather, school, rubber boots, and no baseball. My guess is it is about the same today for an eight-year-old in Fort Worth, except for the bare feet, and everything is a lot more organized.

Of course, everyone remembers and is selective about their past, the good times and bad, all mixed up and jumbled together, and you grab the memory that works best for you at the time, and the right trigger can often rearrange these memories in funny ways. Maybe true, maybe not, but when it's nearly seventy years ago and everyone's pretty much dead or forgotten, the accuracy may not be all that important. If it's true in your head and it doesn't hurt anyone else, there shouldn't be a problem. Absolute accuracy is important in science or launching a space telescope. It is less crucial when recalling a baseball game that may or may not have taken place seventy years ago or who scored the winning run or stole home in a cloud of dust.

Proust wrote about how the taste of a morsel of madeleine taken with hot tea was all it took to cause thousands of remembrances of things past to tumble from his memory, just as a quick glance at a photograph of Ty Cobb on my office wall does the same for me. Clearly, my tastes are not as refined as Proust's, but mine are still bubbling around in my head and Proust's are confined to a printed page, etched in stone, while mine can be altered if required. If I remember something else, and sometimes late at night when it's very quiet I do, I scribble my remembrance on the always-handy yellow pad, in the never-quite-dark bedroom because of the streetlights on Broadway, because I know the thought will have vanished by morning.

When I recall my first encounters with baseball the memories are only good, and I have magnified these happy times over the years and probably successfully suppressed anything bad that may have happened to me. I must have committed horrible fielding errors, struck out with the bases loaded many times, or let our only ball go through my open legs into the weeds and bull nettles to be lost forever or, even worse, let it go into the street and down into a bottomless sewer. But I don't remember the horrors or even the days it rained. I just remember the long sunny days when I had but one thing on my mind: to find someone, anyone, to catch the baseball I always had in my hand, someone who'd not only catch it but who'd throw it back and let me hurl it at them again.

Baseball began for me when I was a toddler in Brownwood, Texas. Some kind person, probably my father, but there's no way to be sure, gave me a small kiddie baseball bat that I probably used to break my other toys. When my father shipped out to the Pacific with his MP Company in 1943, and my mother and I moved from one small Texas town to another, Brownwood to Denton, it was left behind on the top shelf of a closet, along with a swell wooden machine gun. All of our possessions were crowded into our car, and there was no room for nonessentials like a tiny baseball bat or a wooden machine gun. I've never forgotten my first abandoned bat; I know it was real because there is a picture of me holding it, and the loss of the bat is about my only lousy baseball memory. It may also be the reason I've always cared more about pitching than hitting.

The abandoned bat on the top shelf may or may not have hindered my baseball development, but the game really began for me in the spring or summer of 1948, when I was seven, just turning eight. But maybe it was the spring of 1949. The exact date isn't important. In the battle between hard fact and hazy memory, memory always wins, particularly if the hazy memory is a good one. It's easy to recall the big impressions; the little events and precise dates may have mattered then, but they don't matter today. I remember that baseball began to matter, and like the baby picture with the long-abandoned bat, there are pictures to prove it.

One recurring memory is of the eight- or nine-year-old ragtag youngsters in my neighborhood, kids just like myself with maybe a nickel or dime a week allowance, sweaty and dirty, hustling on a weed-infested dusty sandlot field in Fort Worth, Texas. It literally was a field, an expansive backyard, wedged into a triangle formed by Blanch Circle, St. Juliet Street, and White Settlement Road. The part of the field closest to White Settlement Road was plowed up every spring and planted with some kind of crop.

In those days we didn't spend one second thinking about Joe DiMaggio and the New York Yankees or anyone else like that. Why should we? How could we have even known about what went on in such faraway places as New York or Boston, or even the other side of town? We were just kids who could barely read, and when we did it was Action Comics or the latest adventures of Roy Rogers or Gene Autry. We didn't read newspapers and didn't know sport magazines even existed and couldn't have bought one if we did.

The closest anyone I knew ever got to the big-time heroics recounted by nostalgic baseball writers these days was when we took our few pennies to Duckworth's store on University

Junior *Hoot* *Slats* *Lucky*

Drive to buy bubblegum and discovered that one brand contained little cardboard pictures of baseball players. We looked at the faces of players with funny names like *Junior* Stephens, *Slats* Marion, *Hoot* Evers, and *Lucky* Lohrke and though they meant nothing to us, the cards were a bonus, so instead of Fleer's Double Bubble we invested in the gum that had the cards. Some of us saved them, kept them in little piles, or thumbtacked them on our bedroom wall, but what we really wanted was the bubblegum to chew while we played our days away. Collecting cards came later, after we learned to read a few more words and mastered enough arithmetic to work out a batting average.

There was another reason the names and faces on the cards didn't mean anything to us: our reality wasn't big-time players in big-time towns, it was our gravel-strewn, sun-baked field in the backyard, where sharp-edged cracks in the earth were a constant danger, places where the toes of the genuinely barefoot Shoeless Joe Jackson Junior fielders and base runners were easily caught. Little League-like fields with bases and grass? Not in the part of town where I lived; our bases were often big rocks or maybe, when we were lucky, a few small boards. There was no grass, just a dirt field surrounded by a tangle of parched weeds spreading in all directions, waiting to gobble up any ball that came their way. Our ball field was a place where half the kids didn't have a glove, and if the scruffy, usually wrapped-in-friction-tape baseball or battered softball got lost in those ever-waiting weeds there was big trouble, because nobody knew how long it might take to come up with a replacement.

All this may sound like tough times, but they weren't. The games were nonstop rough-house fun because none of us knew anything better, and there were always enough eager kids to organize a game of scrub, a seemingly endless game that could go on for hours, especially on days that weren't too blazing hot. On some of these sizzling Texas days, when those yawning cracks in the black earth seemed to widen like tiny earthquake faults before our eyes, some of our clearly overprotective parents would haul their sunburned and beaten kids inside and the game would be temporarily called on account of sunshine. They were watching out for polio, which they suspected might lurk in the sunshine of our neighborhood, waiting to take advantage of a fatigued young body.

My parents were the most cautious in our part of town, or so I thought, and when confined indoors during the hottest part of the day, I'd prowl about our apartment like a caged lion, hoping for an early dinner, a meal that never came soon enough. After scarcely chewing my last gulp of food, I'd dash into the barely cooler, late-afternoon or early-evening air with my mother's shouts of "wait thirty minutes for your supper to settle" ringing in my ears and, as if by magic, in a flash a dozen kids would pick up where we'd left off, playing with every ounce of energy we possessed until lack of light shut us down, whether our suppers had settled or not. I never saw anyone with an upset stomach, and to the best of my knowledge, none of my playmates got polio except for a little girl across the street. She died, and it scared us all silly, but we still kept playing every day all day, and when the sun went down we started thinking about the next day.

We weren't good players; we were sloppy and untrained. None of us knew what we were doing, and there was no organized play anywhere, even at school. My school, Crestwood, was a fairly new, well-built elementary school that was an easy walk from home down White Settlement Road. I'm told it burned down a few years ago, and that's a pity. No second chance to see it again, but there's still a photograph or two. My third-grade teacher, Miss Christiansen, knew nothing about baseball other than it was her job to hand out a bat and ball at recess, so there was no organized baseball instruction at school, but it turned out I was a little luckier than some of my pals.

Third and fourth grades and the summer in between were my real years of unorganized baseball. In those years football was the main game kids played in Texas and probably still is. I had my own plastic helmet and shoulder pads and football and a jersey and pants. Some of my friends had the same, and we'd play pick-up games in the winter and fall on the same fields we played baseball in the summer but, except for when my father took me to see TCU play SMU at the big university stadium, spring and summertime baseball was what really mattered.

My father was back from the war and a thirty-eight-year-old sophomore at Texas Christian University. He'd been around, had combat medals to prove it, and some of the younger students were suitably impressed with his experience and no-nonsense attitude. A couple of his new, much younger friends happened to be on the TCU baseball team, and one of them gave me my first real baseball instruction. While I listened to a young college player, one of my relatives also gave me encouragement.

My grandfather, Curtis Austin Christian, better known as C. A., was well into his sixties when I first learned of his baseball exploits. My mother had told me stories he'd told her about playing baseball around Georgia, in his home town of Macon, and as far away as

Royston, a small town in the northeast part of the state, all before the Turn of the Century. She convinced me he'd been a great player, and she was certain he could help me become much better, a star in my own backyard, so I looked forward to his visits.

Grandfather C. A. told me he'd been a pitcher and a pretty good one; he threw the ball in a funny underhand way that was a standard delivery in those days, but he threw it very hard, hard enough to play on a couple of good Georgia teams. That was good enough for me, and at sixty-plus he could catch anything I could throw at him, and catching his funny underhand pitch stung my ungloved hand. I didn't think about it then, but I think about it now that I'm many years older than he was in 1947-48. How his arm must have ached. He was in no kind of condition to throw a ball that hard or for that long. But he made the effort, and I was grateful then and still am to this day.

On most spring days I'd walk home from school, but sometimes I'd come outside and spy our ancient battered Chrysler sitting at the curb. This meant not only a ride home, but also a trip to the university to pick up my dad. I'd run up the sidewalk, hop in the car and beg my mom to drive by the TCU baseball field. I knew if I could get her to drive by the field, it would be a cinch to get her to stop, which meant I could watch the TCU baseball stars practice and on occasion do battle with such arch-enemies as the Baylor Bears or Rice Owls while waiting for my dad's classes to let out. The players had the letters "TCU" stitched in purple on their uniforms, but sometimes the uniforms had the word "Frogs" across the chest, short for the Horned Frogs.

I always wondered why anyone would want to be called the "Horned Frogs." The other teams that came to play had much better names, except those terrible Arkansas Razorbacks, and what was a razorback anyway, I wondered in those days. But I worried about things closer to home even more: why were the locals saddled with "Horned Frogs"?

These ugly little lizards ran wild in our part of Texas. They were easy to catch, and I often confined many of them in elaborate sandcastles I built in my backyard sand box and watched them run races up parapets, hoping to escape, which they usually managed to do. But you don't name a baseball team after an unattractive lizard, or so I thought. Yet I always forgot about the silly name when I sat down in temporary bleachers that had been set up alongside the playing field.

Sitting on those slick wooden boards I just watched and wondered how things would turn out, marveling at the way the grownups could throw a ball so fast, hit it so hard, and run so quickly. What made the difference? Maybe it was the big bats they swung so mightily at new, pure-white baseballs, or perhaps it was the ill-fitting, washed once too often, not quite white, not quite gray uniforms. It never occurred to me it might be they were ten times stronger than I was, and at least a hundred pounds heavier. I would sit there watching and wondering until my mother would tell me it was time to go and fetch my father, whom we'd always find waiting patiently, smoking a Lucky Strike, lost in thought about now and then, and thinking about how he would manage to catch up with those years lost to World War II.

⊱ LOCAL HEROES ⊰

I never saw a complete game, never saw the Frogs or the Horned Frogs beat or even lose to anyone, because my father always had to hurry home to have dinner so he could return in time for his always-trying-to-catch-up-and-get-even night classes. Despite this, I got to watch the teenage-plus TCU students in bits and pieces and what I saw was glorious. Then one day, my father, probably feeling guilty about all the abbreviated afternoon games, told me he was going to take me to a real ballpark, at night no less, to see a game from start to finish, and my excitement was almost unbearable.

The better TCU players weren't always in class or vanquishing a Southwest Conference rival; some played for one of the many semipro teams in Fort Worth which were sponsored by local businesses. The teams were made up of college whiz kids, former high school heroes who'd forsaken more schooling for a job, war-seasoned youngsters who loved to play ball, and veterans who'd probably washed out of the Class C East Texas League, and at twenty-five or twenty-six, were certified over-the-hill old-timers. My father's friends played on a team called "Turf Bar," and this was the team I saw that night.

I didn't know what a bar was; if the name had been "Turf Saloon" something might have clicked because I'd seen saloons in cowboy movies. But "bar" meant nothing. The sponsor may have been horrible, Turf Bar may have been a rough and dirty establishment, a place where a decent young student from a Christian-oriented university wouldn't dare be seen, but to me it was just a name, though a name that looked wonderful on perfect white uniforms with red and blue trim.

Those white uniforms seemed to glow under the floodlights illuminating that ball field in Rockwood Park near the Trinity River, just like they glow in those soft-focus baseball memory movies like *The Natural*. This first game and those that followed were my first experiences watching any sporting event outdoors after dark, and they meant a lot to me since my next best nighttime activity was catching lightning bugs and putting them in a jelly jar. No more chasing bugs; here were bright lights, lots of action, people cheering, and a nickel to buy what I remember as the sweetest cherry snow cone in the world.

Sometimes the same teams played on Sunday afternoon in another local park close to home, and while not as exciting as games at night, these Sunday games were perfect for family outings. Strange as it might seem, these semipro games in public parks were the only organized games I ever saw from start to finish for many years, but they made a strong impression because the quality of play was probably good by any standard and, of course, outstanding to my childish eyes.

JIM NOLAN, *Third Base*   JOHNNY JONES, *First Base*
JIM BOYD, *Shortstop*

The two Turf Bar players my father knew both had professional careers: Jim Nolan, an infielder, got as far as the Double-A New Orleans Pelicans, and Jim Busby, an outfielder, had a fine thirteen-year career with various teams in the American League and coached for years, mainly in the American League, until he died in 1996. I don't know what happened to Jim Nolan, but Busby may have already been signed to the White Sox when I saw him, just tuning up for bigger and better things, getting ready to trade in Turf Bar and TCU uniforms for something that said Chicago or White Sox.

These games were thrilling, but they couldn't match what I felt when I was given my first real baseball, plus a bat and beat-up old glove, all courtesy of my personal hero, the TCU/Turf Bar third baseman, Jim Nolan. In today's vernacular, everything but the ball was "game-used." I reused the bat and glove regularly, hopefully with modest distinction, but they were lost or discarded long ago. All that remains are two photographs of me using each, posing with the bat in the backyard and with the glove and a softball in the front.

I still have the now scuffed and yellowing ball that was only used in the front yard on special days to play catch with Nolan or my grandfather. It was used one time too often, but accumulating those scuff marks was worth it then and worth it now. The neat handwritten pen and ink signature that once clearly read "Jim Nolan" is a bit faint these days, but those games of catch only erased his name from the surface of the ball. The memories are intact.

I don't remember the day he gave me all the equipment, but I remember clearly a Sunday afternoon with the two Jims in the park when a hot and sweaty Jim Busby asked if he could have a drink of my cool frosty Coke, and I couldn't hand it to him fast enough, not like that oh-so-cute kid in the Pepsi commercial that ran all over network television a couple of decades ago. A few years after the encounter in the park I was startled to see Busby's face looking up at me from a pack of just-opened bubblegum cards. "Hey! I know that guy; he drank my Coke in Fort Worth!" But none of my friends believed me.

I was only eight or nine but glowed with pride as he gulped it down; it never occurred to me he'd be a famous major league player. He already was an important player to me, a larger-than-life figure in my small world. Nolan played catch with me; Busby drank my Coke. This was big-time stuff to someone who'd never even seen the Double-A Fort Worth Cats in action. And I never did; they played too far from home and my father was too busy studying. The Fort Worth Cats and the struggles in the bigs weren't important. What mattered to me were daring deeds done close to home, like a guy from Turf Bar crushing one into the darkness, past the outfielders and the lights, maybe as far as the Trinity River. I suspect it was the same for most kids my age in small American towns and even cities like Fort Worth.

• Outfielder Jim Busby

JIM BUSBY

In 1947, Jim Busby was a standout on the TCU baseball team. He was featured in the 1948 college yearbook with a full-page picture that confused me. I didn't realize the picture showed him after he'd completed his swing; I thought this was the way he stood as he waited for a pitch. I remember trying to match the position in the front yard with no success, while generating lots of laughter from any grown up who might be looking. I was only seven going on eight and had a lot to learn.

Busby and his teammate Jim Nolan were kind to me when I was a child, and baseball turned out to be pretty good for Busby. He had a long and distinguished career, as a player and a coach, with many different teams. He had a thirteen-year career as an exceptional outfielder. He was an adequate hitter and an outstanding base runner. He coached for many years, primarily working with Paul Richards, and in his later years was associated with Houston in various capacities. He had a twenty-eight-year career in Major League Baseball, including thirteen as an active player.

The glove I used throughout my high school years was a Wilson Jim Busby model. I look at it today, and the gigantic gloves in use dwarf it. In fact, the gloves on the hands of Little Leaguers today are far larger, but it worked okay in the mid-1950s, and if I had the opportunity to use it in 2020, I'm sure it would be just fine. I'm certain it would perform far better than I.

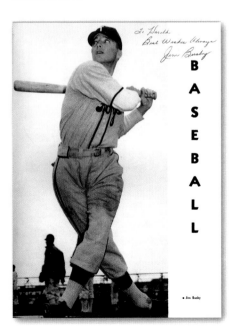

MORE LOCAL HEROES

Sporting events of all sorts in the America of 2020 are far more important than they were in 1947 or 1957, especially from a financial standpoint. The viewership of a single Little League World Series game on ESPN surpasses the number of fans in the stands for all seven World Series games in 1947. The New York Yankees and Brooklyn Dodgers drew 389,763 fans. The year 1947 was the first year an entire World Series was televised, and it was estimated that all seven games had a total viewership of 3.9 million. The television rights that year cost $65,000. In 2020 the cost will be in the billions. The final game of the 2020 Little League World Series will have millions of viewers, and ESPN will pay many millions of dollars to televise the children's baseball championships. They are willing to do this not because they are interested in nurturing young athletes but because there is an audience for children's baseball games.

Some years ago, Donald Honig wrote a lovely book entitled *Baseball When the Grass Was Green*. There is still plenty of green, more than ever, but it isn't the grass that is greener. It is the piles of cash that are being generated.

Of course, baseball and other games aren't really very important. The folks who peddle the sixty-second spots at millions per second for the Super Bowl would have you believe otherwise, and it is true that morons in Central America have actually gone to war over soccer matches, but in the overall scheme of things the games don't matter much, except maybe at the moment when they're happening, especially if you are a playing participant, which is what I longed to be. Sporting events won't change the world, but sometimes a grandly heroic feat in a game can leave just as big an impression as an occurrence of truly earth-shattering magnitude.

I don't know about anyone else, but in my memory there were two "shots heard round the world" in the twentieth century, and my guess is that more people of a certain age remember Bobby Thompson's home run blast than remember the bullet fired by Gavrilo Princip in 1914. One "shot" won a baseball game in 1951; the other started the chain of events that led to World War I. There's no doubt which one was the more significant, but I have little doubt which "shot" is more meaningfully etched in most American minds, at least minds who know about baseball. Even now, nearly seventy years later.

No, baseball isn't really *that* important in the overall scheme of things, but it made a difference to me when my worldview was very small, and I felt more passionate about baseball, playing the game or, when I couldn't, which was most of the time, watching others play it or reading about it in magazines. I suspect it did the same for many other kids in those years, both those down the street and thousands of miles away.

Maybe baseball is still important to some kids who play just for the fun of it or even those who dream of playing in the Little League World Series and later having a career in baseball. But kids who can spend a hundred dollars for a baseball autographed by a perfectly average player or even buy complete sets of bubblegum cards are unlike anyone I knew in 1950.

Thank goodness.

I only had one autograph and a handful of bubblegum cards in those days, but all those sandlot skirmishes, cherry snow cones, and nighttime games where everyone in a uniform seemed as heroic as Roy Hobbs made a difference in my life. I have to believe that buying bubblegum cards by the pound or autographs out of catalogs doesn't have the same meaning to a nine-year-old today, that the same passionate feelings can't be there when it's just buying and selling. This is just commerce; there's a big difference in buying an official baseball in a store and catching one in the stands, or better still, being handed one by a real player you admire.

Looking back on it today I wonder if what happened in those few years was just foolish, starry-eyed nonsense, why all those very commonplace, ordinary events meant so much, and still do. I don't think my parents or anyone else I knew realized how much I cared, how much it meant to me. The truth, or at least the truth I choose to remember, is that what happened in the last couple of years of the 1940s into the early 1950s, the forces of the game, the players, my friends, and the times, convinced me that baseball was the most important thing in my life, and for the rest of my childhood, and well into high school, playing the game was almost all that mattered. It was, of course, just a wonderful fantasy, the foolish dreams of a kid growing up, but I lived the dream to its utmost and it became the basis of this story.

I played whenever or wherever with anyone who was available. When polio epidemics forced kids off the playgrounds and makeshift ball fields during the hottest parts of the summer days, I read over again and again the tattered baseball magazines I'd accumulated and organized my bubblegum cards over and over, forever rounding the card's corners and diminishing their value in today's marketplace. I can still remember some of the stats I etched into my memory on a hot afternoon almost seventy years ago, and on that same day, if not reading, organizing, or memorizing, I probably played baseball board games with similarly throttled kids.

I remember one in the late 1940s called Ethan Allen's All Star Baseball, a game with little discs, spinners, and plastic pieces that, depending on where the spinner stopped, made their way around a cardboard baseball field or back to the dugout. The discs were named

for famous players of the 1920s-40s. The disc was divided into sections, and if the spinner landed on "1," it was a home run. There were sections for singles, doubles, fly outs, strikeouts, and all the rest. Allegedly, the size of the sections was based on actual statistics. Babe Ruth had the largest section for home runs, Ty Cobb had the most singles, and I seem to recall Rogers Hornsby had the most doubles.

Most of my baseball treasures survived countless moves from Texas to Indiana to New York, but somehow the All Star Baseball game was misplaced or more likely thrown away because it had become so worn and threadbare. I had forgotten all about it until I saw one at a flea market in the 1960s, bought it for a few dollars, and was transported back a couple of decades, but now it also had players who had emerged in the 1950s.

As I'd read a baseball magazine, make a pile of cards, or play the All Star Baseball game with a friend, I'd also keep my eye on the patch of shade by the apartment house next door. I'd wait until it was about eight feet wide, and then it was time to make my move on Manager Mom. Eight feet wide and about sixty feet long, plenty of room for two kids to throw a ball back and forth, and if a third guy was handy, it was enough room for a mock base path and a fierce game of pickle.

My begging and pleading would interrupt my imagined jail keeper as she was concentrating on the travails of *Just Plain Bill* or the heartbreak of *The Romance of Helen Trent*, and with half an ear she'd hear me promise to stay out of the direct sun, that nobody ever got polio from playing catch or even pickle in the shade, it was just when you played too hard in the sun, got overheated that bad things happened, when you might become crippled for life, never to play again. I was such a pest, or maybe because she was such a softie, most of the time I got my way, and as soon as I did, I'd dash out of my living room dugout onto a shady make-believe base path.

I must have been right about the shade because polio never grabbed me, but at night, if my leg hurt a little, for whatever reason, I was terrified. All sorts of horrors bubbled around in my head while I lay motionless in my bedroom and wondered if this was how polio started. Would I be crippled by morning? My friend across the street had died of the disease, and I'd lie awake, wondering if maybe I'd played just a little too hard. Somehow, sleep always came, and as the morning light filled my bedroom the demons vanished as quickly as my real or imagined pain, and it was time for another day of baseball and, when necessary, dodging the sun.

Our games in the backyard field were haphazard affairs. I don't think any of my playmates ever played anywhere else in those years, even at school. And by those years I mean the spring of 1948 though the summer of 1949. I know there was no baseball field or backstop at Crestwood; it was just a schoolhouse surrounded by grass and asphalt. I have an old photograph of that backyard field, and it is weed-covered from left to right and top to bottom. But somehow we managed very nicely.

THE OTHER SIDE OF
✿ THE TRACKS ✿

Those sunny days in Texas came to an abrupt end in August 1950, when my mother, father, and I got in our now decade-old Chrysler with a rented trailer attached, left Fort Worth, and headed north to Bloomington, a small city in southern Indiana, where my father would continue to chase his education and a much-hoped-for job. But the first stop was a bedroom in a log cabin located on a dirt road overlooking the frequently flooded Salt Creek. The bedroom was in the home of my mother's sister, Martha. She and her husband Roy T. Will had invited us to camp out in their spare bedroom while my parents waited for married students' housing to open up at the University of Indiana.

From the log cabin on Yellowwood Lake Road, my parents transported me to Nashville, population about five hundred, enrolled me in the fifth grade of the local school that was housed in a building that was very old where I felt very young, certainly younger than the kids in the other half of my homeroom, who were all in the sixth grade. The school was grades one through twelve, but there weren't enough rooms for each grade to get one of their own.

I was only in Nashville for a semester and never saw a baseball; the season was long over for me and everyone else. In this new part of the world, the only round ball that mattered in southern Indiana had to do with one that was aimed at an overhead basket, something I'd never seen before. I'd heard of basketball and actually thrown a basketball, not at a basket but at someone else, dodgeball style, but had never played the game or even seen a basketball court.

School began later in Nashville than in Texas, sometime in mid-late September, because the children were needed to help harvest crops. I rode a yellow-orange school bus to school every morning for over three months, and I remember freezing some mornings waiting for the bus by the bridge that spanned Salt Creek. The bus was okay, but it had been much more fun during corn-picking time, riding in the bump-along wagon dodging ears of corn while one of the Shepard brothers, the farmers down the road, navigated their tractor and corn-picker machine through their fields next to the creek.

One day one of the brothers let me drive the tractor, and I was a grown-up ten-year-old for a minute, and about the same time my father gave me more training with my .22

Remington in a ravine next to the log cabin. I did well enough that he let me fire his 9mm German Luger twice, and I hit the target both times. It was the first and last time I ever fired a handgun.

School in Nashville was interesting. The two main things I remember from those days were that my classmates were very rural and not interested in school, and this puzzled me. The kids in Texas loved school. I also remember my lesson book, a tablet actually with an Indian in a feathered headdress on the cover. It was filled with inexpensive, easily smeared lined paper, and I had to use a straight pen dipped in ink from an inkwell that was imbedded in the upper right-hand corner of my antique desk. Lefties didn't stand a chance. The instructor for the fifth and sixth grades was Mr. Percival, and I don't remember anything about him other than I later learned a gang of overaged and angry grade-schoolers had beaten him to a pulp for some reason or another.

Thankfully, I wasn't in Nashville very long. In January of early 1951 an apartment became available in the married student housing provided by the University of Indiana. My father rented another trailer and headed west on Highway 46 towards Bloomington. He knew the way. While the school bus hauled me to Nashville he drove in the other direction for a day of classes.

In those days, married graduate students were housed at Hoosier Courts on a first come, first served basis or as apartments became available. The apartments were in converted World War II-vintage wooden army barracks, with eight families to a building. It was a Spartan bare-bulb-in-the-ceiling one-smelly-gas-heater-for-the-entire-place kind of apartment, but hundreds of other families lived in identical circumstances, and while the living conditions were dreary, no one starved, and a dollar a day was affordable.

Imagination is a wonderful thing, and in my muddled mind I was certain I was better off than some of the other kids in the neighborhood because our tiny apartment overlooked what appeared to be a large baseball field—at least I thought it was a baseball field. The snow was a foot deep when we arrived, and after our trailer of household items was unloaded into our new home, I buckled on my rubber boots and made my way through the snow drifts to the corner of the field and inspected what seemed to be a shabby, falling-down backstop, haphazardly made of old clothesline poles and chicken wire. A year or so later, after I'd won a camera at the grocery store raffle, I took an out-of-focus snapshot. It may not have been much, but that backstop growing out of the snow made my soon-to-be-eleven-year-old imagination run wild about what kind of a playing field might be revealed in a few months when the snow vanished. Maybe there was something green under all that snow!

Anticipation didn't melt the snow, but as the temperature crept upward the expanse of white eventually turned into mottled-brown field of grass and mud. As the days raced toward summer and the weather warmed the grass seemed to grow an inch every day, and suddenly a man on a tractor towing a mowing machine appeared, and before my barely believing eyes, he transformed the field into an almost ready-to-be-played-on pasture of heaven. At least it seemed that way to me, because I was used to a weed and bull nettle ravaged, gravel-strewn, toe grabbing sun-cracked hot lot.

The season began immediately as balls and gloves came out of closets and bats from under every kid's bed. A gang of a dozen kids about my age claimed the field as their own, a place where I was to spend two glorious summers. If baseball had been good on a rock-strewn, arid, sun-baked semi-pasture in Texas, it was positively spectacular playing on that lush green backyard Hoosier Courts field in a neighborhood where it seemed everyone had a bat and ball and a glove, wanted to play, and was willing to work at it.

We patched the backstop, came up with makeshift bases, worked on base paths, and someone even found a beat-up old home plate that was reverently installed, befitting its undoubted former glory. If a playing field and an endless supply of players weren't enough, providence glanced in our direction and led us to an almost endless supply of broken bats, serviceable baseballs, and some coaching as well.

This is the first picture I ever took with my Brownie Hawkeye. I later became a better photographer, but my ability as a baseball player remained about the same.

An east/west railroad was the southern border of our housing development; the tracks were also the Bloomington city limits, and we were on what was assumed to be the wrong side of them. The only immediate effects of our lack of citizenship were that we had no easy access to the city school system and were banished from local Little League teams, but the railroad that put us outside the city did have some positive effects.

The fifteen-foot embankment that served as a roadbed also served as a fine left (and partial center) field boundary for our homemade ballpark. More importantly, the tracks were ideal for various adventures and games when we weren't playing baseball. The gigantic puffing 4-8-4 Northern engines thundered out of the west shaking the ground of our ball field, and all play ceased as we all stood in wonder and watched them rumble by pulling what seemed to be hundreds of freight cars. Who wouldn't have been thrilled by these mighty steam engines—grown-up, real-life examples of the trains we saw in the colorful American Flyer and Lionel wish books, trains that we dreamed of finding under the Christmas tree but never did? All the action stopped and we'd stand silently, watching the seemingly endless freight trains that rumbled by two or three times an afternoon.

One day a group of us took a baseball break after a train had just rumbled by. We gathered our courage and walked west on the roadbed, wondering where the tracks might lead us. We had all been repeatedly warned by our parents about playing on the tracks, that they were dangerous, but we bravely took our young lives in our still mostly tiny hands and ventured farther and farther away from the safety of Hoosier Courts. We didn't venture too far, but as the days passed we became ever emboldened, walking farther from the safety of our playing field and edging closer and closer to the city with each outing.

We discovered the tracks had been cut through limestone, and digging and blasting had left many cave-like openings in the steep but not unclimbable cliffs. After a few days of simply hiding in the caves like a would-be Jesse James and his gang of train robbers, some-one suggested that we climb to the top of the cliffs to look down on the train and dream of jumping onto the boxcars, just like Lash LaRue or Wild Bill Elliot did every Saturday after-noon at the picture show. A fine idea we all thought, and we carefully made our way to the top, never once considering that a false step or a loose stone would send a climber crashing down the cliff onto the tracks.

No one fell, and memory fails in recalling who reached the top first, but whoever it was found not a spot to rob a train but rather the outer reaches of the practice field for the Indiana University baseball team. We pulled ourselves over the edge and were stunned to see grownup players running around in uniforms, and it didn't take much scheming on anyone's part to devise a way to use this discovery to our advantage. The fantasy of a great train robbery was quickly pushed aside for the reality of more immediately useful treasure.

We soon found an easier route to the practice field, and after school it was always our first stop. With glove in hand, each one of use would make ourselves as useful as possible, chasing fouls, looking for balls in the weeds, or we'd cast our gloves aside and carry water or act as batboys. We would do anything to stay close to the field and the players. And, as we suspected, rewards quickly came our way. We had all the broken bats we could carry, beat-up baseballs were stuffed in our pockets, and many balls, not too badly used, but "lost" in the weeds and carefully "overlooked" by us during practice, were suddenly discovered as soon as the university players left.

The cracked bats we were given were far too large for any of us, but we used them anyway. Just the names on them were an inspiration. A few nails, some friction tape, and we could swing a bat that had a name on it like Babe Ruth, Lou Gehrig, or Rogers Hornsby.

Old, repaired Louisville Sluggers were genuine treasures; my favorite was a lumbering Rogers Hornsby model I fixed up. It was much too heavy, and my still-small hands could barely grip its fat handle, but I tried to use it just the same. My baseball-throwing grandfather had always told me my hands were so small he was surprised I could even hold a baseball, and now I was trying to grip an enormous bat. The Hornsby model was thirty-six inches long, and unless someone threw the ball very slowly, I couldn't get it around in time to even bingle a grounder into right field. Yet how I tried, and how embarrassed I was that I had to use a thirty-four-inch bat with a skinny handle if I really wanted to give the ball a smack.

It was a glorious summer, one that ended much too soon, and in September I learned baseball was not really the game of choice in Bloomington when, for the first time, my gym instructors thrust an Indiana basketball into my uncertain Texas hands. A new game to learn; it was okay I thought, but I couldn't wait for spring, to be outdoors, playing on the big green field in my backyard. And it literally was in my backyard. Building 22 was the closest building to the field. My future in baseball was destined, or so I thought, even if I didn't know what "destined" meant.

The snow was once more covering the ground when 1952 arrived, but time passed, the snow melted, the grass turned green, and we were ready to play again, but there was something new on the horizon that year at the local grocery store.

In March or April someone discovered new, giant-sized packets of bubblegum cards in the candy racks. This was the first year the large Topps cards were issued, the ones that sometimes sell these days for hundreds of thousands of dollars or more for a complete set. In 1952 it was a nickel at any grocery and the surprise of seeing Gil Hodges or Andy Pafko pop out.

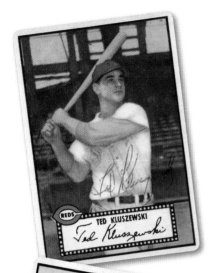

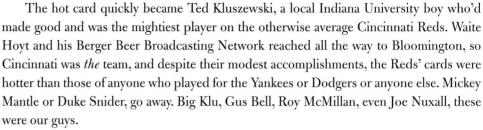

The hot card quickly became Ted Kluszewski, a local Indiana University boy who'd made good and was the mightiest player on the otherwise average Cincinnati Reds. Waite Hoyt and his Berger Beer Broadcasting Network reached all the way to Bloomington, so Cincinnati was *the* team, and despite their modest accomplishments, the Reds' cards were hotter than those of anyone who played for the Yankees or Dodgers or anyone else. Mickey Mantle or Duke Snider, go away. Big Klu, Gus Bell, Roy McMillan, even Joe Nuxall, these were our guys.

That year was much like the year before, and when the university team shut down for the summer our new supply of bats and balls dried up, but we'd managed to stockpile enough to make it through the summer. We also ventured across the tracks to do battle with assorted townies. We were never so happy as the day we thrashed one of the Little League teams in a decidedly "unofficial" contest. We were not allowed to join a Little League team because we lived on the other side of the tracks, outside the city limits. My parents even had to pay $25 or so tuition for me to go to the McCalla school on the "right" side of the tracks.

Our glee at beating the fancy-pants uniformed Little Leaguers was short lived. A week or so later some tough kids from another part of town ventured across the tracks onto our home turf and throttled us. One big kid named Ike was the outsider's superstar. He was a couple of years older and a head taller than most of us. I can still remember exactly what he looked like, right down to his badly deformed ear, but I mainly remember he hit a ball I pitched to him over the railroad embankment, the only time it ever happened. This was an incredible feat in my eyes; I was pitching and throwing what I thought was my best twelve-year-old stuff. Ike hit me like I was a schoolgirl or a fancy-pants Little Leaguer.

I was humbled but impressed, and despite occasional disasters this was the best summer of unorganized baseball I ever had, the last time I lived with a couple of dozen good kids my own age, all of whom had a glove on their belt and a bat on their shoulder, ready to play at a moment's notice. My family stayed in Indiana for the rest of the year and into 1953, but we moved to New York before I could spend another full season on that wonderful handmade ball field on the right side of the tracks. My father had secured a job in Syracuse, New York, and we headed east in August.

AUGUST 21, 1953

We headed east from Bloomington, crossed into Ohio, headed northeast on Highway 42, and could have found a way to bypass Cleveland, but my parents had a surprise in store. A slight detour was in order, and on a Friday afternoon in August we found ourselves in Cleveland. We found Highway 20, headed east, and picked out an inexpensive motel somewhere on Euclid Avenue, where my mother would spend a lonely evening glued to the radio while my father and I ventured back to the gigantic 78,000 seat Municipal Stadium, where the Cleveland Indians planned to battle the always cellar-dwelling St. Louis Browns in a twilight double header.

Cleveland was the largest city I had ever visited. It had over 900,000 Indians fans in those days. It was three times as big as Fort Worth. In 2020 it doesn't even have 400,000, and Fort Worth is nearly three times as big. Things change.

It was also the largest baseball stadium in the country, certainly the largest I would ever see. I bought a program. It cost a dime, and that included a little pencil to fill in the boxes on the scorecard. I also bought an inexpensive felt pennant that had the names of all the current players, an envelope filled with pictures of all the players, and, finally, a little patch to sew on a jacket or a sweatshirt that featured the now politically incorrect Wahoo insignia. I could barely contain myself. And this only became worse as the game began, because Bob Feller was scheduled to pitch the first game, which he did.

Feller pitched a complete game and Cleveland won, 7-3. Al Rosen hit two home runs, and, as I recall, he hit another in the second game, which Cleveland won, but I can't prove it because it never occurred to me I'd need a second program to keep score for the second game. And it didn't occur to me that in 2020 there would be something called the internet where in about ten seconds I could find that Cleveland won the second game, 3-2, scoring the winning run in the bottom of the twelfth inning off Harry Brecheen, sometimes known as *The Cat*, but not that night.

We weren't in the front row; we were pretty far back but on the first level, on the first base side. There was a clear view of all the action and the action started fast, because in the first inning Wally Westlake, subbing for Larry Doby, walked, and Al Rosen hit his first home run of the night. Two to nothing at the end of the first inning; Cleveland was ahead, and Bob Feller made sure they stayed ahead. Way off in the distance I could see Satchel Paige sitting on his rocking chair, but he didn't pitch in either game. I'm so glad I didn't see him lose that second game in relief, but had he been in maybe the Brownies would have prevailed.

BOB FELLER

Bob Feller pitched and won the first Major League game I saw in person. It was against the lowly St. Louis Browns on August 21, 1953. It was just serendipity; we were on our way from Bloomington, Indiana, to my father's new job in Syracuse, New York. It wasn't the most direct route to Syracuse, but it was close enough, and my thoughtful parents timed it perfectly for me to see one game in Cleveland. It just so happened that Feller was pitching, and that made my day. He was my favorite pitcher in the entire world, and for reasons I no longer remember, Cleveland was my favorite team.

A couple of months later I wrote him a letter and asked for an autograph, sending along a color picture from a sports magazine and perhaps a card and a slip of paper. I may have even sent along the program from the ballgame; it is autographed and I know I didn't get it at the game. I may have written him again. There are other autographed items in my scrapbook, but my guess is the letter to Feller was the first I wrote.

The large color picture came back and is dated 10/9/53. It hung on my bedroom wall in a cheap Woolworth frame until I graduated from high school, and then it was retired to various attics until it was "saved" when I assembled all my teenage memorabilia, some years later.

Bob Feller was perhaps the finest pitcher of his era. He didn't win three hundred games, but he would have if he hadn't served four years with the US Navy in the middle of his ca-

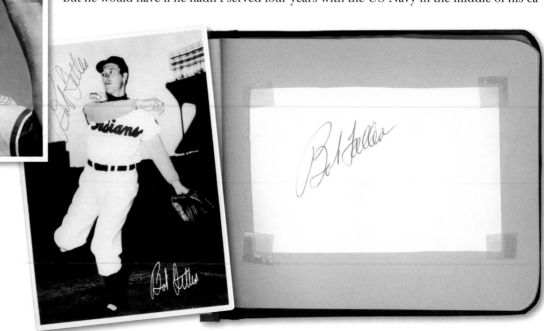

ST. LOUIS	1	2	3	4	5	6	7	8	9	10	AB	R	H	PO	A	E
19 KOKOS, lf		0					0				4	0	0	4	0	0
6 HUNTER, ss	0	0	5.0								4	0	0	1	3	0
16 KRYHOSKI, 1b	0		H.R	0		5.0					4	1	1	2	1	0
20 WERTZ, rf	2.b		0	0		H.R					4	1	2	1	0	0
40 STEPHENS, 3b	1.b	0	0		1b						4	0	3	0	3	0
11 COURTNEY, c	0	1b		0	0						4	1	1	6	0	0
5 YOUNG, 2b		1b		0	0						4	0	1	7	0	0
3 GROTH, cf Dyck	0	0		0							3	0	0	1	1	0
Littlefield		5.9	0		0						3	0	2	1	0	0
											34	3	8	24	9	0

4 MARION, mgr.   14 LENHARDT, of   24 TURLEY, p   32 CRANDALL, coach
7 SIEVERS, 1b   15 EDWARDS, of   26 STUART, p   33 CAIN, p
8 DYCK, 3b   18 LITTLEFIELD, p   27 LARSEN, p   34 BERRY, ss
10 MOSS, c   22 KRETLOW, p   29 PAIGE, p   44 SCHEFFING, coach
12 PILLETTE, p   23 BLYZKA, p   31 BRECHEEN, p

CLEVELAND	1	2	3	4	5	6	7	8	9	10	AB	R	H	PO	A	E
32 SMITH, rf Simpson		5.9	0	W4.0							3	0	1	5	0	0
1 AVILA, 2b	0	1b	8.0								4	2	2	2	2	0
14 DOBY, cf Westlake	W	1b									4	1	1	2	0	0
7 ROSEN, 3b	H.R	W									4	2	3	2	1	0
3 MITCHELL, lf Kennedy		0	W								2	0	0	2	0	0
4 HEGAN, c 15 GINSBERG, c		1b	0	1b	5.0						4	1	2	4	0	0
6 GLYNN, 1b	5.b	1b	W		1b	5.0					4	1	2	8	0	0
2 STRICKLAND, ss	0		0	W	W						3	0	0	3	3	0
W.Feller p	0										4	0	0	0	0	0
	5.9										31	7	11	27	7	0

5 MAJESKI, 3b   12 BRISSIE, p   25 GARCIA, p   35 SIMPSON, rf
8 FRIEND, 2b   18 TIPTON, c   26 HOOPER, p   40 LOBE, coach
9 EASTER, 1b   19 FELLER, p   27 WIGHT, p   42 KRESS, coach
10 LOPEZ, mgr.   21 R. LEMON, p   31 WESTLAKE, of   43 HARDER, coach
11 HOUTTEMAN, p   22 HOSKINS, p   33 KENNEDY, rf   44 CUCCINELLO, coach
24 WYNN, p

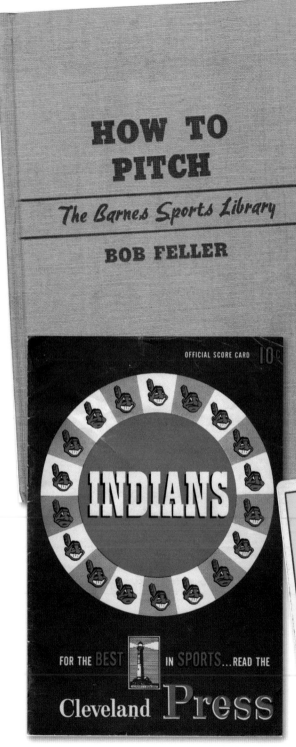

reer. In 1941 he won twenty-five games; in 1946 he won twenty-six. It seems likely he would have done about as well during the four years he missed. Even so, his numbers are impressive, and between the years 1939 and 1952 he was regularly in first place in wins, complete games, strikeouts, innings pitched, and shutouts. In 1946, the year he returned from the US Navy, he led both leagues in wins (26), games (48), complete games (36), innings pitched (371), strikeouts (348), and shutouts (10).

Fast-forward a few decades. In 1988 I was producing a music event on the SS *Norway*, an ocean liner once known as the SS *France*. There was also a weekly sports program on board that featured a celebrated athlete. This week turned out to be Bob Feller's week on the high seas. I was lost in my own production and I first encountered my childhood idol when I turned a corner on a day at sea and spotted the cruise director conducting a pseudo athletic competition, one that involved the sport's celebrity of the week seeing how fast he could run while holding a volleyball between his knees. It turned out Bob Feller couldn't run very fast holding that kind of ball. I was embarrassed for him, but he turned out to be a very cordial, intelligent guy, who was friendly to everyone who approached him. I actually managed to sit down with him for a moment on a beach in the Bahamas. Somehow he'd managed to secure a day or two old edition of the *New York Times* and was busy reading it when I interrupted him. He looked up, we chatted, and he couldn't have been nicer. This didn't surprise me at all. He'd been nice to me thirty-five years earlier in 1953.

TWO LOST
SUMMERS

Except for the games in Cleveland, the move from Indiana to Syracuse, New York, ruined my summer in 1953. I was miserable because I had to leave my friends in Hoosier Courts, and my only consolation was that Syracuse had a Triple-A baseball team, which offered the possibility of seeing some almost major league games played by former and soon-to-be major leaguers. I didn't know it then, but the move ended my sandlot career; if I'd known I'd never play baseball again, except as part of an organized, uniformed team, I might have chained myself to our old broken-down backstop. But how could I have known what was in store for me? It didn't take me very long to find out once I began to walk around my new neighborhood.

That first year in Syracuse was a horror; our modest apartment at 321 Kenwood Avenue wasn't so bad, but I was terribly lonely. Since we arrived toward the end of the summer I didn't have any chance to meet other kids at school. At first I imagined that would come later; somewhere there had to be carloads of kids just like myself who wanted to play baseball all day, but I was dead wrong.

It turned out I wasn't just the new kid on the block; my block was in the wrong part of town. The kids on the north side of Syracuse seemed more interested in casing parking lots than playing on sandlots, and their sport of choice, at least in those years, was petty larceny. I don't think I swung a bat once that summer in Syracuse; all that was available was an occasional game on television, bubblegum cards, fan magazines, and keeping my eye on one of my neighbors.

The neighbor was a grizzled old man of at least thirty-four who lived three doors away at 315. He was an ancient (to me), former major league player, now hustling at second base or wherever he was needed on a given day, for the Syracuse Chiefs. His name was Ben Zientara. The local papers usually referred to him as Bennie but I was much too shy to call him anything at all. He'd had a brief major league career, beginning with Cincinnati in 1941. World War II interrupted his playing days, but he came back for a couple of years before being sent down in 1949, washed up at the age of twenty-eight, never to be in the majors again. He was a gruff but friendly man, a hero to me just because he was a real ballplayer. He may well have been the glue that held the Syracuse team together, and the following year he became a hero for the entire team, but that's another story.

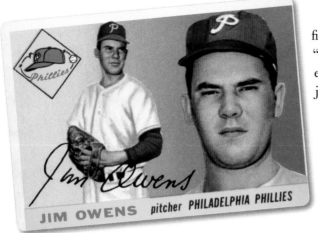

JIM OWENS pitcher PHILADELPHIA PHILLIES

The Syracuse Chiefs, a Philadelphia Phillies farm team with no certifiable stars, were managed by a former Boston Red Sox infielder, Lamar "Skeeter" Newsome. The manager of a Triple-A team does not have an enviable task because someone else always has first call on his players, and just when a hitter gets hot or a pitcher finds the groove, the telephone call from Philadelphia comes in and it's back to the drawing board to try and patch together another lineup or create an entirely new team. A few of the guys shipped south to the Phillies hung on and had modest careers, but most were back in Syracuse in a few weeks, or before the end of the season, hoping they could regain their position in the lineup.

The 1953 team was not very good; they wound up next to last that year, but they were an honest to goodness Triple-A baseball team with a typical mixture of players. About half of them were "older" men, decent players like Bennie Zientara, who'd been in the majors but would never be there again; the other half were youngsters, most of whom would have a brief fling with Philadelphia or some other National League team. One pitcher, Jack Sanford, actually had a fine career that lasted a dozen years, winning twenty-four games in 1962 for San Francisco, but most of the players were up and down, usually down. Sometimes they were called up at the right time and found their face on a bubblegum card or in a baseball magazine, but that didn't make for much of a career.

I was a twelve- going on thirteen-year-old innocent that year, dreaming of baseball because I had no opportunity to play it myself, and limited opportunity to see it played by anyone else. I didn't realize it then, when it was happening, but baseball was very different in 1953 and in many ways almost as innocent as I, at least by today's standards. There were no agents, few scandals, no performance-enhancing drugs, no interminable inter-league playoffs; plastic playing fields were unknown, nitwits at networks didn't dictate the starting time of the World Series, and Dizzy Dean could be heard singing the "Wabash Cannonball" on most Saturday afternoons, courtesy of some local station.

Many of the guys who played the game may have been heroes in the summer, but in the winter, they were just middle-class, ordinary folks who worked in sporting goods stores or automobile dealerships or other such places. They weren't worshipped; their egos weren't pumped up every day. A handful of stars were celebrated, but not too many, and even they were accessible. It was a good time to love the game, all the mystery and excitement surrounding it, and an even better time to gather bubblegum cards, a few at a time, and try to complete a set. When your entire life is only a dozen seasons long and you don't know any better, bubblegum cards matter.

If someone could complete a set, and my goodness how I tried, it meant something, a real accomplishment; it meant you had determination, that you could out-trade, outtalk, out-flip, or outwit anyone who had the cards you needed. You didn't have to out-spend anyone because there wasn't anyone to outspend, and if there had been, they didn't have any more nickels than I did. You didn't go to a store and buy a complete set in an embossed can, and there weren't a dozen sets issued every year, just one or two.

It wasn't a business yet, just fun. There was no such thing as buying cards in quantity, and if there had been, no one I knew could have afforded it. Anyway, that was just commerce, and in my innocent unformed mind, baseball wasn't about spending money. No self-respecting kid my age, someone who lived and breathed baseball, would even consort with a fat and indolent boob with a big allowance who couldn't play, but who could just buy up cards instead of getting them fair and square, a nickel or two at a time. People like that were only good for one thing: they were marks to be taken advantage of and beaten out of their cards at every opportunity.

Cards, autographs, a hat, or other treasures given to you by a ballplayer—these weren't things to be bought and sold; they were objects that made you part of a game you loved to play, small mementos that meant a great deal, and they meant even more when there weren't many opportunities to play yourself. These assorted bits of memorabilia were to be found, worked for, and obtained by being clever. Of course, money did change hands sometimes, but when it did, it was more than just a business transaction.

I remember when I first discovered that baseball cards didn't start with the first ones I had seen in 1948 and that they'd actually been around for years. I tracked down a kid who had some from the 1930s. Some former occupant had glued them to his bedroom wall. Somehow I managed to get them off the wall and traded him something for them. They were beat up, but they were old, and I thought they were terrific.

G. BROWN, CHICAGO NAT'L

OLD BASEBALL CARDS

A year or so later I discovered that in the early days of this century, very beautiful, carefully made cards came in packages of cigarettes. In those years I guess grown-ups collected the cards and gave them to kids, but the ones I saw and liked best were issued around 1910. It was a real challenge to find someone who had any for sale or trade, and I don't remember how I found him, but somehow I tracked down Wirt Gammon, a man who had some, and it turned out they cost a dime apiece.

The number of dimes I had was directly related to how hard I was willing to work at collecting newspapers and bottles and selling newspapers to the scrap dealer or redeeming bottles at the corner grocery. When I had enough dimes for a five-dollar check I'd give it to my mother and the check would make its way to Tennessee and Gammon would send me fifty cards. And the cards were not just ordinary players, but often famous Hall of Fame players like Cy Young or Ed Walsh and Walter Johnson and even Ty Cobb. He sent me two Ty Cobb cards, but that wasn't what excited me about those cigarette cards. The excitement came from them being so very old and extremely attractive. Some of the most attractive were of people I'd never heard of; all I knew were the names at the bottom and a team. It would be many years until I had a book where the obscure player's names appeared.

Those old cigarette cards are now hot commodities and have been for years. A Honus Wagner has sold over and over again, for upwards of a million dollars, maybe more by 2020. Even more commonplace cards are sold for many hundreds by rotund bearded dealers who seal them in plastic and grade them. Not only are the status of the players important, like whether or not they are in the Hall of Fame, but the cigarette brand on the back of the card makes a difference. The cards could be found in twenty or so different kinds of cigarettes; most that I had were from the most popular brands like Piedmont and Sweet Caporal, but if the card had a Hindu or Lenox or the scarcest, Ty Cobb, it was worth substantially more.

Of course I knew none of this at the time, and the old Ty Cobb cards I got with my hard-earned dimes are worth far more than one I might purchase for a thousand dollars from some dealer or at a Sotheby's or Heritage auction in 2020 because they're real, they were earned. The cards that celebrities and "investors" buy for hundreds of thousands of dollars are just like artificial playing surfaces, air-conditioned stadiums, and glass-enclosed luxury boxes bulging with servants and too much food. They are phonies. Sure, they are what they are, perfect-condition mementos, forever sealed in plastic, untouched by a child's sticky fingers. But these cards have no back-story, no history. A perfect cigarette card from 1910 didn't thrill a dozen kids along the way; perhaps it thrilled a well-heeled collector in 2020, but there's a big difference.

M. BROWN, CHICAGO NAT'L

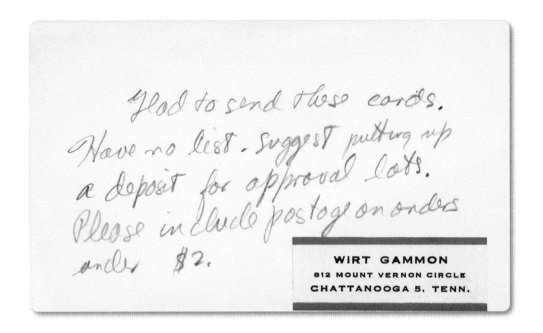

Had to send these cards. Have no list. Suggest putting up a deposit for approval lots. Please include postage on orders under $2.

WIRT GAMMON
812 MOUNT VERNON CIRCLE
CHATTANOOGA 5, TENN.

This may be an uncomplicated, overly sentimental, innocent way of looking at what is now a very big business for many dealers, but I don't doubt for a minute that the way it was in 1953 is the way it should be forever. It's a sad thing when greedy grown-ups try to buy up children's dreams and then sell the dreams back to them at a profit.

Think about the dealer's concept of "game used" equipment, which they claim is much more valuable than something that is new in a box. Why is a game-used ball any better than a kid-used bubblegum card? One that was lovingly collected in some manner, bought, traded, or flipped, and maybe became worn a little over the years. Not something that was hidden away, never adored, but now still has perfectly sharp corners, hermetically sealed and "graded." It doesn't pass the smell test. At least it doesn't with me.

MACARTHUR STADIUM

In the spring of 1954, my life in baseball was a little better, but only because of other people playing. I'd survived half a year at "stolen hubcap" junior high and looked forward to the day when Ben Zientara began gearing up for another year with the Chiefs. I'd discovered that the Chiefs played at an old 1930s-vintage ballpark not far from where I lived and maybe, with any kind of luck, I might get to go to some games and see him play with his teammates.

I managed to get an occasional hello out of Zientara over the winter, and I hoped that he might even consent to toss a ball in my direction when the weather warmed. I started to hang out in front of his apartment. I'd toss a ball in the air, run around in circles, and finally catch it. If he ever noticed me at all I'm sure he viewed me as the village idiot. I didn't consider my behavior in any way bizarre, but it didn't work. Zientara never had anything to do with me, but one day when he was in a charitable mood he suggested I should come out to the ballpark and watch him play. I turned emotional cartwheels and then managed to parlay his casual suggestion into an "invitation," and with it convince my gullible parents I'd been asked by our neighbor to attend a game.

Chiefs 1954

FRONT ROW—l to r—John Blatnik of, Ben Zientara inf, Bob Micelotto ss, Manager Skeeter Newsome, Marvin Blaylock 1b, Larry Novak of, Jack Spring p, Bobby Bach batboy.
MIDDLE ROW—l to r—Trainer Al Ritter, Kent Peterson p, Don Richmond of, Lou Heyman c, Ed Zinker p, Ed Mierkowicz of, Bob Bowman of, Jim Command inf, Ben Tompkins inf,
BACK ROW—l to r—Joe Erautt c, Forest Smith 3b, Lyn Lovenguth p, Joe Lonnett c, Marvin Williams p, Jack Meyer p, Jim Owens p, Joe Tully p, Jack Sanford p.

1954 OFFICIAL Chiefs SCORE BOOK 10¢

MacARTHUR Stadium

71st International League Season

1954 OFFICIAL Chiefs

MacARTHUR Stadium

71st International League Season

YOUR FAVORITE ★ Autographs

Marv Blaylock
Bob Bowman
Don ...berg

"Skeeter" Newsom
Jim Owens

ROSTER

	B	T	Wgt	Hgt	Age	Residence	1953 Club
PITCHERS							
... Arthur L.	R	R	183	5:11½	30	Gary, Indiana	Syracuse
..., Lynn R.	L	R	170	5:10	30	Camden, N. Y.	Syracuse
...hn R.	R	R	175	6:01	22	Medford Lakes, N. J.	Schenectady
...James P.	R	R	195	6:00	20	Gifford, Pa.	Terre Haute
...Kent F.	R	L	170	5:10½	28	Salt Lake City, Utah	Phillies-Balt.
Sanford, John	R	R	175	5:11	24	Wellesley, Mass.	Baltimore
Spring, Jack E.	R	L	173	6:01	21	Spokane, Wash.	Spokane
Tully, Joseph O.	R	R	195	6:01	26	Tucson, Ariz.	Albany
Williams, Marvin W.	L	L	168	5:10	24	Dearborn, Mich.	Syracuse
Zinker, Edward J.	R	R	197	6:04	24	Chicago Heights, Ill.	Schenectady
CATCHERS							
Erautt, Joseph M.	R	R	170	5:08½	32	Portland	Buffalo
Heyman, Louis W.	R	R	225	6:02½	29	Wausau, Wisc.	Terre Haute
Lonnett, Joseph P.	RL	R	180	5:10	27	Beaver Falls, Pa.	Baltimore
INFIELDERS							
Blaylock, Marvin E.		L	175	...1½	24	Ft. Smith, Ark.	Minneapolis-Syr.
						New Orleans, La.	Baltimore
						...yde Park, N. Y.	Kansas City

ROSTER

	B	T	Wgt	Hgt	Age	Residence	
PITCHERS							
Dyck, Arthur E.	R	R	185	6:04½	28	Jefferson City, Mo.	Bea...
Hartley, Arthur L.	R	L	183	5:11½	29	Gary, Ind.	Sy...
Landeck, Arnold A.	R	R	190	6:01	27	Peotone, Ill.	Buffalo-Sy...
Lovenguth, Lynn R.	L	R	170	5:10½	29	Camden, N. Y.	Te...
Markell, Harry	R	R	209	6:01½	31	Bronx, N. Y.	Sy...
Robinson, John E.	R	R	190	6:02	23	Cedar Grove, N. J.	Sy...
Williams, Marvin W.	L	L	168	5:10	24	Dearborn, Mich.	Sy...
Griffore, John F.	L	R	190	5:11½	32	Saginaw, Mich.	Ly...
Krieger, Kurt F.	R	R	201	6:03	26	St. Louis, Mo.	
CATCHERS							
Drescher, William C.	L	R	190	6:02	30	Haverstraw, N. Y.	Kans...
Partee, Roy R.	R	R	180	5:10	34	Sun Valley, Calif.	
Kinaman, Richard C.	R	R	201	6:00	28	Sacramento-Okla. City-Indian...	
INFIELDERS							
Blaylock, Marvin E.	L	L	175	6:1½	23	Fort Smith, Ark.	Chicago Minn...
Rodriguez, Hector	R	R	165	5:07	31	Havana, Cuba	Chicago
Verdi, Frank M.	R	R	170	5:10½	27	Brooklyn	Binghamton-Kans...
Zientara, Ben	R	R	170	5:09	33	Chicago, Ill.	Sp...
Lamanna, Frank			195	6:02	33	Syracuse, N. Y.	
OUTFIELDERS							
Blatnik, John	R	R	205	6:00½	31	Lansing, Ohio	Rochester
Gillenwater, Carden E.	R	R	168	6:01½	34	Fountain City, Tenn.	
Welaj, John L., Jr.	RR	L	160	5:11½	37	Arlington, Va.	
Workman, Henry K.		R	185	6:00	27	Los Angeles, Calif.	
Schult, Arthur W.	R	R	210	6:03	25	Scarsdale, N. Y.	

1954 OFFICIAL Chiefs SCORE BOOK 10¢

MacARTHUR Stadium

71st International League Season

1954 OFFICIAL Chiefs SCORE BOOK 10¢

MacARTHUR Stadium

71st International League Season

BEN ZIENTARA

Highlighting SPORTS
By Jack Slattery

A man who has contributed largely to the success of the Syracuse Chiefs thus far in the season is veteran Ben Zientara. Ben was the object of much MacArthur Stadium abuse over the '53 season simply because he was one of the "ole folks" whom the fans tired of seeing.

Not only has Ben done a great job for the Chiefs this year, but he has done it quietly and conscientiously, not looking for or calling attention to his contributions. Though the fans had no personal animosity toward Ben nor Corky Corbitt nor Carden Gillenwater they certainly were rough on the trio of vets though these three did nothing but play their best and do all in their power to make the Chiefs a winner. Something they just could not be last year.

When a back ailment made it impossible for the veteran catcher Bill Drescher to help the Chiefs behind the plate and at bat Bill was released and Zientara selected to replace him as coach.

Undefeated Manager

ONLY A FEW NIGHTS LATER Manager Skeeter Newsome was thumbed from a game and Zientara took over for Skeeter who was fuming in the clubhouse. And only minutes later Ben made a really important decision. Though it was early in the game, Ben chose to pull the starting pitcher and put himself in to bat with three runners on base and two outs.

He promptly belted a safe blow that scored two runners and put the Chiefs back into the ball game. They went on to win and his Chief teammates toasted him as the winningest manager in baseball. As a matter of fact, he is. Since that time he again replaced Newsome and the Chiefs came out on top, giving Ben a two and zero record as skipper.

The remarkable thing about Ben's ability to come out of the dugout or coaching box and step in and deliver all-important hits is that his coaching duties frequently make it impossible for him to get a chance to take any practice in the batting cage before the games.

In spite of that, Ben has four hits in six pinch-hitting tries for a very respectable .800 average. On May 20 against Richmond Ben struck out batting for Jim Owens and the Chiefs lost, 3-1. On June 10, he singled in a pinch-hitting role and the Chiefs defeated Buffalo, 3-6. Against Richmond on June 25 he singled and Syracuse won, 6-5. Two days later against the same club he again singled and the game ended in a 2-2 deadlock.

On the second of this month he doubled to plate three runners and the Chiefs drubbed Buffalo, 10-3. The next day he walked as pinch-hitter and Buffalo won, 1-0.

Broken down as regular and pinch-hitter this is the way Ben has tormented clubs throughout the league. He's two for two against Buffalo; two for four against Richmond; six for 18 against Ottawa; zero for two against Montreal and zero for one against Havana. Ben hasn't played in games with Rochester and Toronto.

Hopes to Become a Manager

BEN IS A VETERAN OF 34 YEARS and Doc Ritter, who remembers him as a brash youngster trying to make the grade with the Cincinnati Reds, says: "There never was a more determined cuss in a baseball suit. In the old days it was worth a rookie's life to dare to step into the batting cage ahead of one of the established performers. But Ben would step in there brandishing his club and soon the old guys, though they never would show it, so liked his spunk that he became one of them. There aren't many youngsters around today with the same zest and love of the game that Ben showed us as a rookie in 1941."

Zientara approaches the game with the same spirit and determination today. And manager Newsome is the first in line when it comes to handing out compliments for his fiery assistant. Ben unhesitatingly spends extra hours with the younger players, doing all in his power to help make them better players in the future and the Chiefs a better team now. Newsome says: "There's no doubt about it, Ben's done a great job for me. I just turn the infielders over to him and don't even give them another thought. Nobody works harder than Ben."

BEN ZIENTARA

Zientara was a star and hero for about a minute with Syracuse in 1954. Some of his exploits are detailed in a yellowing article by Jack Slattery that I saved after it appeared in the *Syracuse Post Standard* that year. But Zientara's exploits were real as the Chiefs struggled to make the playoffs and finally nudge their way into the Little World Series with Louisville.

The newspaper headline for the playoff game with Havana read "Hero Role Split By Lovenguth and Zientara." Zientara had four hits in five tries that night. A few nights later he had three hits in the victory that eliminated the Toronto Maple Leafs. The paper said, "Bennie Zientara, who has been playing grand ball over the past month got three hits in five trips to lead both clubs tonight."

I don't know what became of Ben Zientara. *The Baseball Encyclopedia* notes he was born in 1920 and died in 1985. He played four seasons with Cincinnati in the 1940s, but missed four years because of World War II. He was only a journeyman player; in four seasons he had 230 hits in 278 games, but he was the first player I ever met who'd played for a major league team and he was nice to me, so I still remember. I hope others do as well.

The Syracuse Chiefs played at MacArthur Stadium. It had been built in 1934 on what seemed to be former wetlands, at the south end of Onondaga Lake, on the north side of Syracuse. It was renamed for General Douglas MacArthur in 1942 and had been enlarged to hold about ten thousand if every seat and bleacher was filled. The lake was once pristine, but even in 1954 it was losing its charm. It was not a place for swimming; only race boats and a regatta made use of its waters. Solvay Process, a chemical plant that produced many tons of sodium carbonate annually, had been dumping its refuse into the lake for years, as had other plants. The city of Syracuse pumped raw sewage into the lake as well, and the result was a lake that was for many years the single most polluted body of water on the east coast. In recent years some efforts have been made to clean it up, and some progress is being made, but it will take a few billion dollars to complete the job.

Best Wishes
Ben Zientara

In 1954 the stadium wasn't in a very good neighborhood. It was mainly industrial, like the aforementioned chemical plant, with a good deal of lower-middle-class housing all around. It was just a twenty-minute walk from our apartment, but I was forbidden to walk; I had to take two buses to reach the ballpark—a trip downtown and then a transfer to the park. It took over an hour instead of a short walk, but I was so eager to go to a game that I offered no argument and was thrilled when I was given bus fare *and* admission.

The first Sunday afternoon there was a home game I took the two buses to a real Triple-A ballgame. I paid my twenty cents and roamed the bleachers that were on the first-base side of the field hoping to catch a foul ball or gathered up my nerve to accost a player and plead for an autograph. The best part was I was on my own, and didn't have to sit with any elderly people like my then forty-year-old parents. I even got an autograph. I found a scrap of paper and borrowed a pencil from someone and Bob Bowman signed it. Bowman, who died in 2017, remained with Syracuse for two years and then was called up by the Philadelphia Phillies, where he had a modest five-year career. He even holds a couple of peculiar major league records.

I couldn't have been happier; I'd made my first trip to the stadium and returned home successfully, so I knew it would be a simple matter to do it again. I just had to come up with the fifty cents I needed for admission and transportation. Somehow I managed to make the trip all summer long, even when we moved to the other side of town after the school semester was over.

I never sat in the grandstand; the bleachers were just fine, and besides, they were right next to the building that served as the clubhouse for both teams, where all the players had to enter the stadium through a small door in the right field wall. I'd position myself just as close to the door as possible, on the other side of the chain-link barrier, and it was easy to slip a piece a paper, a bubblegum card, or a program through the fence and ask for an autograph.

I even had a beat-up old camera courtesy of a kindly next-door neighbor and managed to take a few snapshots of the players; when I'd get my out-of-focus, poorly composed results back from the drugstore I'd ask the players to sign them, and they never complained. They were never less than cordial; they'd pose and seem genuinely pleased to be asked to sign something, particularly a bubblegum card. It seemed they all loved doing what they were doing, even in Syracuse. They appeared enthusiastic, and I'm sure the players I chased sensed I felt they were special because to me they were special. The entire process was simple and very sincere. This is how simple it was in 1954 and how it worked.

To reach MacArthur Stadium I had to take one bus downtown and transfer to another that stopped at the stadium. This was a long ride, well over an hour, and after we moved to the other side of town near the university, it was even longer. The result was I spent a lot of time on buses, but this wasn't such a bad thing. I returned from the ballpark exactly the same way, except there was one very important difference. Many of the players, particularly those on the opposing teams, had to take the same city bus to their hotels downtown. It may have been there was no other transportation for the opposing team, or a taxi was too expensive, but the bus downtown was often jammed with ballplayers.

For my plan to work it was very important to make certain I was on the right bus. I'd watch the bus stop at the clubhouse door, time my entry, and as often as not I'd share a seat with someone I'd just seen on the field a few minutes before. The young players were trying to make their way to the relative safety of the Onondaga Hotel on Warren Street. Sitting next to a Triple-A player was serious stuff to a thirteen-year-old, and if I was lucky I'd be able to chat up a twenty-year-old second baseman that played for Montreal or an outfielder like Clint Hartung who used to be with the Giants but was now with Havana, and probably drive them crazy for half an hour. If I was sitting next to someone it was a cinch to get a good autograph, maybe even a "best wishes" or an inscription to me personally. It's funny; in those days I always told them my name was Harold; I never used Hank. I don't remember why.

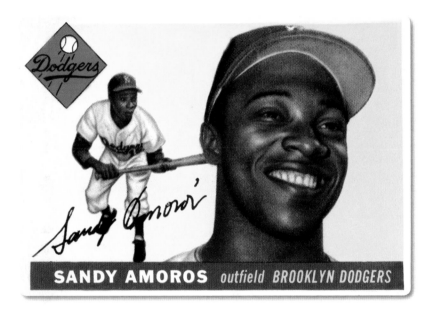

As the summer wore on I gathered my courage and even made my way into the Onondaga Hotel to seek out players who might be lounging in the big chairs in the lobby. I once cornered Roberto Clemente and Sandy Amoros sitting together when Montreal was in town, and I remember these two guys, who were only twenty and twenty-four respectively, seemed so much older than the Syracuse players. They didn't say much, maybe their English wasn't so good, but they signed everything I thrust in their direction and were friendly to a silly kid in hostile territory. It really was that simple.

THE OTHER SIDE OF TOWN

Our new home on the south side of town was anything but hostile but very different from the neighborhood I'd just left. The only problem was I was a new kid on yet another new block, and unfortunately the block was still in the middle of a baseball wasteland. It seemed all my neighbors were old folks, childless or infirm. There were no sandlots, no organized or unorganized ball in my part of town. And once again, because we'd moved in the summer, I didn't know anyone and wouldn't until the school semester began.

All I had was the garage wall; I was reduced to throwing a ball at a rectangle I'd drawn on the garage wall or, when I was very lucky, a game of catch with my father who'd been a semipro catcher in his youth and even had a CCC baseball team under his command in the 1930s. Most of the time, however, he was tired and overworked, so it was just the garage wall and me; throw three or four balls, go pick them up and throw them again. It's amazing how low one can sink; there's nothing much lower than playing a game with a garage wall. Spring might have been the cruelest month in that other wasteland, but a lonely August in my barren backyard, staring at a bumpy rock wall, wasn't much better. And the balls didn't even bounce back. They just hit with a dull clump and slid down the wall. In 2020, the garage wall is still there but, thankfully, my chalked rectangle is gone.

That summer there was one other pastime other than the wall and commuting to MacArthur Stadium: writing to famous players. I'd pestered my folks incessantly about visiting the Baseball Hall of Fame in Cooperstown that summer, and I'd come away from the shrine with starry eyes and handfuls of postcards and assorted memorabilia that seemed well-suited for autographs. My new challenge became to see if I could get these cards signed by the great old timers in the Hall of Fame. I had no idea where any of them lived and was sufficiently unimaginative to think of anything else, so I trudged off to the public library and began searching in out-of-town telephone books. My fourteen-year-old mind rationalized that if someone had played in Philadelphia he might still live there. I didn't have much luck; I think the only one I found was Pie Traynor, who still lived in Pittsburgh.

Discouraged, I changed my plan and began to concentrate on writing to active players, care of their ball clubs, and the results were immediate and astounding. Autographs on photographs, bubblegum cards, and slips of paper began to flood into the old milk box on the back porch that served as our mailbox. Sometimes a kind player would send a postcard-sized photograph of himself if his club supplied them. Cleveland had crisp, glossy black-and-whites; the Yankees furnished their players with color postcards; the St. Louis Cardinals' postcards were black-and-white, poorly printed and inexpensive, but each had a little note on the front and a place for the player to sign. Almost all the clubs had a standard postcard in the summer of 1954, and regardless of color or quality, all of them were exciting to a fourteen-year-old fan.

Meanwhile, the hometown Chiefs were chugging along, sometimes in the first division, sometimes out but always scrapping their way to a decent number of wins, and I kept making my way across town to spend the afternoons in the bleachers when the boys were home. My autograph book became crammed with blue ballpoint signatures, the International League stars of the day, sandwiched in next to the big-league stars who'd answered my letters and, at least in memory, almost all of those to whom I wrote replied.

I look at those old autograph books today in amazement; there is one slip of paper on each page, sometimes with a small photograph or a bubblegum card stuck down on the facing page, and it's remarkable to see just how many did respond, often with a "best wishes" or "kindest regards." As often as not it was the famous players who wrote an extra salutation, a Joe DiMaggio, Mickey Mantle, or Ted Williams.

The summer ended with my favorites, the Cleveland Indians, taking first place in the American League with a record number of wins, and for the first time in my short life my favorite team won something. The locals ended the season tied for fourth place with Havana, and this created havoc in the International League. Montreal and Rochester had a secure spot in the playoffs, but a single game between Syracuse and Havana would determine who

Joyous Chiefs Welcomed on Return from Triumph in Toronto

Police Escort Greets Tribe; Leads Parade

Pair of Road Games Slated This Weekend

Pennant Chases

INTERNATIONAL LEAGUE
(Semi-Final Playoffs)
Syracuse eliminated Toronto, 4 games to 2.

Results Yesterday
Montreal 4, Rochester 3 (Montreal wins best-of-seven series, 4-2).

Game Saturday
Syracuse at Montreal, night.

NATIONAL LEAGUE

	W	L	Pct.	GB
New York	95	55	.633	—
Brooklyn	89	65	.589	6½
x-Milwaukee	86	64	.573	9
x-Cincinnati	74	77	.490	21½
Philadelphia	73	77	.487	22

would meet the Toronto Maple Leafs in the International League playoffs. All eyes, particularly mine, were diverted from the American and National Leagues to a single game at MacArthur Stadium.

The game with Havana wasn't much of a contest; I didn't get to go since it was on a school night, but I listened as 4,671 fans at the stadium cheered the team to a 13-4 victory. To make it even better, my former neighbor, Ben Zientara, was the hero of the game, with four hits, including a home run. He was carried off the field on the shoulders of his much younger teammates. Then came the series with Toronto.

To the amazement of everyone, the hustling Chiefs beat the league-leading Toronto, four games to two; in the final game Zientara was three for five. Baseball fever was rampant in Syracuse by now, and thousands of fans greeted the team at the New York Central train station when they arrived. I wonder how long it has been since any returning Triple-A team has been greeted by a thousand fans or any fans at all, at a train station or even an airport or a bus station.

But in September 1954 the players were piled into open cars and paraded through downtown with a police escort. It was as if they'd already won all the marbles, but within a week they'd won some more of them. They beat the much superior Roberto Clemente-led Montreal four games to one, and suddenly the Chiefs were the toast of the town, their victories trumpeted on the front pages of both local newspapers, the *Herald Journal* and the *Post Standard*.

The locals had been playing a little over their heads for well over a month, and now they found themselves in what was known as the Little World Series to determine the champion, the best team in the International League against the best of the American Association. The Chiefs gave the Louisville Colonels a good shot, but they finally ran out of gas. Even though it was a school night I managed to see game four at the stadium; it was the last one Syracuse won, and it was a great game, a 1-0 two-hit victory, a pitchers' game.

I remember two other things about the game. I froze that night, along with the four thousand-plus other fans. The guy with the blanket concession made a couple of month's rent with that game. I also remember walking out of MacArthur Stadium that night thinking how wonderful it would be to play in a real stadium, even one in Syracuse, built on a swamp. I was growing up a little and beginning to realize I'd never be Bob Feller, and for me MacArthur Stadium looked just fine. Of course, Bob Feller wouldn't get to be a hero again; the Giants had whipped the Indians in four straight, and he hadn't even gotten in a game.

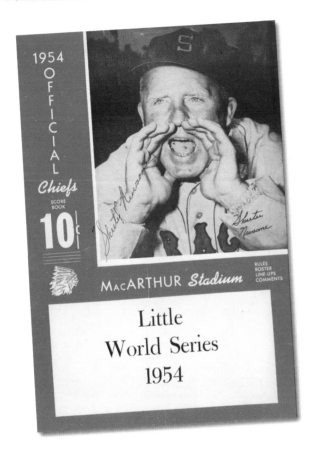

The season was over, and the only baseball activity left to me was pursuing ball players through the mail or, occasionally, in person. One of the first I encountered was George LeRoy Wiltse, better known as "Hooks."

HOOKS WILTSE

Hooks Wiltse was the first old-time baseball player I ever met. He may have been the oldest person I had ever met; he was about seventy-five at the time. I don't remember all the details, but I somehow got next to him and secured an autograph on September 18, 1954, about the time Syracuse was fighting to win a place in the International League playoffs. Later, I heard him speak at a gathering of the Hot Stove League, and he signed another slip of paper. He was stronger the first time I asked; maybe answering all the questions tired him out. I don't remember anything he said that night, but I do remember that when I had an opportunity to get old baseball cards I made it a point to look for ones that featured him, and eventually found three.

Wiltse was active for a dozen years around the turn of the century, primarily with the New York Giants. He had a few sensational seasons and once pitched a ten-inning no hitter. He was also an outstanding defensive player; his nickname came from the way he "hooked" ground balls, and he sometimes filled in at first base when it was required. He played professionally until the age of forty-six.

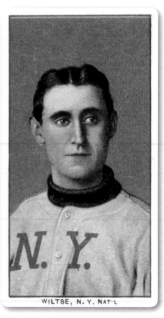

⮞ NEW PEN PALS ⮜

My season as an observer and super fan was over. I had been regularly uprooted for the past couple of years, moving here and there as my father chased his education and jobs, but that fall I found myself in a new school with every prospect of having four years of high school in one location. My first day at William Nottingham High School even started out pretty well; I noticed a large display case that held championship trophies celebrating the glories of past baseball teams. It seemed they did something at Nottingham other than prep kids for reform school.

I was a lowly freshman and knew the likelihood of making a varsity team as a fourteen-year-old was unlikely. Of course I dreamed of making the baseball team, but the odds were not in my favor. Still, I was determined to make the team the following spring, if for no other reason than I was fed up with lonely afternoons with the garage wall. Nothing was more important than making the team, but while I was waiting to take the field there was no harm in keeping in touch with as many old-time and current players as possible via the US mails. After all, there were better odds of getting a letter from one of the Cleveland Indians than finding a pick-up game or someone who even played baseball in my neighborhood.

The first person that responded to me with an actual letter was Duke Markell, a journeyman pitcher who'd been with Syracuse in 1953, but was with Rochester in 1954.

DUKE MARKELL

I don't know if Duke Markell was a star with the Syracuse Chiefs in 1953, but for some reason, he seemed special to me. He wasn't on the team in 1954; he was with Rochester that year, but I remembered him and wrote him a letter in January 1955. He responded with a warm letter and enclosed a photograph of himself, possibly in a Rochester uniform. But I was thrilled to get the letter and the picture, and even more thrilled with his inscription.

Harry Duquesne Markell was born in Paris, France, in 1923. He is barely a major league footnote; he was with the St. Louis Browns for about a minute in 1951, appearing in five games. He won one and lost one; not a bad record, considering he was with the lowliest team in the Major Leagues. But it didn't matter; it wasn't good enough for him to stick around or hook up with anyone else.

The elegant-looking letter from Markell was thrilling, but I was primarily interested in the old-timers, and my main target was Ty Cobb. My maternal grandfather, Curtis Christian, the same one who'd played catch with me in Texas just a few years earlier, had played with Cobb when they were teenagers in Georgia, so I felt a special affinity for The Georgia Peach, a man I regarded as the greatest living player. I had read many stories about him, that he was a wicked, mean-spirited man who cheated and would do anything legal or illegal to win a game, but none of these horrors came through in the stories my grandfather told of playing with him at the turn of the century.

Ty Cobb, first row, far left-hand side. My grandfather, Curtis A. Christian, holding baseball, first row, second from right.

My grandfather told me Cobb, who was a few years younger, was a scrappy kid who played hard but fair, and he was very proud he was recognizable in a photograph that accompanied a *Life* Magazine article Cobb had written. The photograph showed them together on a team in Royston, Georgia. Well, I thought, my grandfather was in the photo, he'd played with Cobb and said he was okay. That was enough; I believed him. He was on the ball field with the man, and all those guys who wrote the books were somewhere else (or not even born). I decided I should try my best to track down Ty Cobb, maybe ask his advice on what I should do to help me make the high school team, and find out for myself if he was so awful.

The public library wasn't much help. I found a T. Cobb living in Detroit and wrote a letter off to him but never heard back. Then I had an idea, one that turned out to be a good one. The Baseball Hall of Fame had to know where all its members lived. Why not ask them? I was ashamed I hadn't thought of this earlier; it would have saved a lot of wasted time at the library. I sent a letter to the Hall of Fame in January 1955, and within a couple of weeks a letter came back from Sid C. Keener, the director. He wrote me a short note and sent the address of every living member, as of June 1954. I was overwhelmed; here was everything I needed to track down not only Ty Cobb, but also everyone else in the Hall of Fame.

In those years there probably weren't many professional autograph collectors, just a lot of kid fans like myself, so it was no big deal to send out a list of addresses. Sid Keener had no reason to be concerned that some crook would try to steal memorabilia from an old player or that a published address would mean thousands of people a week would descend on old Cy Young. It was just a simpler time. Thank goodness, or I'd never have found Ty Cobb.

It took me a week or so to get a letter off to Ty Cobb in Menlo Park, California. It's now over sixty years later and I'm embarrassed my letter is so badly written, that I didn't include an envelope complete with a stamp (which I usually did) for him to use in reply. I was naïve, ill-informed, and inconsiderate, all those things, but something in my letter must have piqued the great man's interest (or maybe I just annoyed him). No matter, he wrote a vigorous response and returned the small Hall of Fame card and the piece of paper I'd enclosed.

I was elated, of course; not only did I have a Ty Cobb autograph but I had a letter from him as well, probably the first letter I'd ever received from anyone other than a blood relative

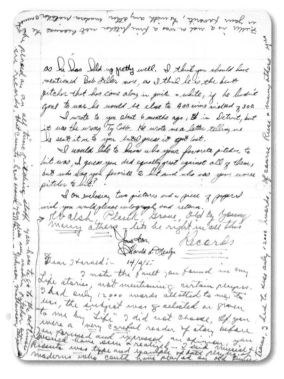

wishing me happy birthday. It didn't matter that he'd written back on the letter I'd sent him. In fact, this made it even better, because it was more personal. This was all the encouragement I needed, and I began to write to others on the Hall of Fame list and the letters started to come back. I recently looked in an old autograph book that begins with Ty Cobb. On succeeding pages, he is followed by Rogers Hornsby, "Home Run" Baker, Tris Speaker, Larry Lajoie, Dizzy Dean, Mel Ott, Frank Frisch, Fred Clarke, and Lefty Grove. That was a pretty good run.

I'd send the players photos from magazines, cards from the Hall of Fame, anything I could find. Some were returned quickly, others took longer, but they almost all came back, neatly signed in ink, even when the players were old and infirm. I remember getting a note from Roy Mack saying his father, Connie, was too fragile to sign autographs, but he sent me a small card he'd signed years before. I sent Frankie Frisch a whole series of photographs of himself; he signed them all and wrote me a letter as well.

Sometime later a letter arrived from Big Ed Walsh. Now these were not just two ordinary guys; as an all-round player there was scarcely anyone better than Frisch in the nineteen years he played, and he was the playing manager of the St. Louis Cardinals for five of those years. Rogers Hornsby is the only other player who played and managed at the same level. Ed Walsh? After fourteen years of pitching for the usually lowly Chicago White Sox, he still holds the lifetime ERA record, an incredible 1.82 runs per game, over fourteen years, a number that will probably not be achieved by any of the current million-dollars-plus-a-year men in any single season of their careers.

I don't remember exactly what I wrote either of the gentlemen, but Frank Frisch took time out from whatever he was doing to write a beautifully encouraging letter, full of the "be a good boy, work hard and you'll get ahead" ethic. This kind of moralizing doesn't hold much weight with the kind of guy who won't play his best unless he makes as much money as his agent or his own ego thinks he deserves, but Frisch's words meant a lot to me in 1955, and their spirit should mean more today than I'm afraid it does. He even throws in a line about not forgetting my studies. I wonder how many of the Major League stars of today and the Hall of Famers of tomorrow worried about their own studies, let alone those of an unknown kid in an upstate New York backwater? Even if they were so inclined, I wonder how many of the $100-an-autograph crowd would or even could sit down and type a letter like The Old Flash?

Ed Walsh's letter was another matter, a letter from someone who had retired before Frank Frisch played a Major League game. The handwriting is from another age, the kind I saw on yellowing letters in the attic, written in the 1800s by long-dead relatives. The letter from Walsh doesn't say much other than he is very proud of what he accomplished as a player. It's possible both Frisch and Walsh were ignored and lonely in 1955, that few letters turned up in their mailboxes, but I doubt it. I think they were just nice people, willing to share a little of themselves with a fourteen-year-old kid. The why is irrelevant; that they wrote the letters, that the letters thrilled me then and in a strange way still do, is all that matters. It makes them live on a little longer and fills me with happy memories.

Then something amazing happened: I came home from school on a cold day in mid-March and found a letter from Ty Cobb waiting for me. I had written to him after I'd received the note from him, apologizing for not having enclosed an envelope and probably addressing some of the points he made in his brief comments. In fact, I suspect I was trying to cover all the errors I'd committed in my first letter as thoroughly as possible, but whatever I'd done worked and, to my amazement, he'd taken the time to reply and not with a hurriedly scribbled note around the margins of letter I'd sent him.

This was a serious five-page response in which he not only answered a couple of things I must have asked him but also strenuously attacked a man named Gene Schor (Schoor), whom he referred to as a "creature," a lovely, dated way to zing his tormentor. I had no idea then, or now, who this "creature" might be, and I didn't care. All that mattered was the five-page letter from a man who was possibly baseball's finest player and certainly its fiercest competitor.

I was simply overwhelmed as I read and reread the letter. I didn't even pay any attention to the two lines at the bottom saying he couldn't write to me anymore. He had taken the time to write something to someone he didn't know, someone he'd probably never know. This from the man who was supposed to be not only the best player, but one who was often reviled as the meanest, nastiest man to ever play the game, who'd hit his mother with a bat if it meant an extra base. Somehow, this didn't add up to me, even as a fourteen-year-old.

The letter was important to me both in the classroom and on the ball field. I was a decent student, but my English teacher was always on my case about some deficiency; my book reports were sloppy or I was reading the wrong book. After Ty Cobb's letter it didn't matter to me if what I had written pleased my teacher or anyone else, but whether or not my words might generate some interest in the mind of some other reader. Miss Freshman English Teacher might have her nouns and verbs under perfect control, but had anything she'd ever written managed to generate a five-page response from anyone like Ty Cobb? I didn't think so, and it was probably at this point I began to understand that perfect grammar and following all the rules didn't necessarily make a writer, it only makes a grammarian, or maybe an English teacher. A few years later my English teacher was Maureen Borah and she let me get away with writing my senior paper about Dizzy Gillespie and she didn't bat an eyelash.

I only had to look at Ty Cobb's letter to prove the point, at least to myself. It was full of mistakes, a D in composition at best, maybe even a failure, but the letter made its point. It wasn't dull, and I understood what Cobb was talking about; it seemed as though he wrote like he played baseball: get from first to second and then to home any way he could and on his own terms. After this dose of Ty Cobb on paper I was much less concerned if I got a B- on a paper about my reaction to *The Yearling* or whatever else I might be asked to write. I may have learned more about writing than baseball from Ty Cobb, but that made no difference at the time.

A THREE-CENT
❧ STAMP ❧

Anyone who thinks that life in general and baseball in particular isn't more complicated and less charming today than half a century ago, needs to look no further than the letter I received on February 1, 1955, from Sid Keener, the director of the National Baseball Hall of Fame and Museum.

I wrote to Mr. Keener all those years ago, in late 1954 or early 1955, because I'd struck out at the public library and had an idea that the Hall of Fame would surely know where its members lived and might be willing to share this information with me.

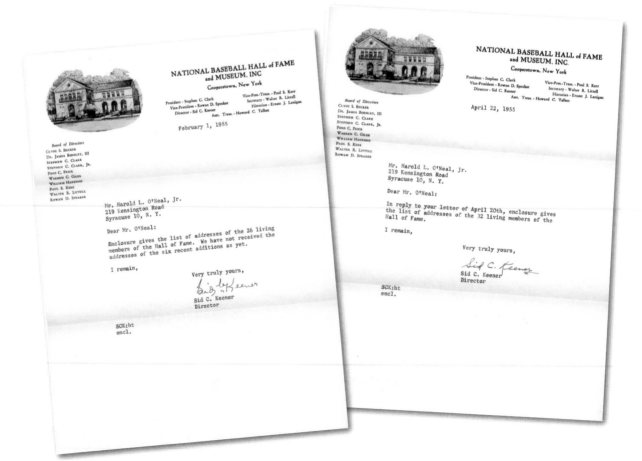

I must have written the right thing because the response from Keener, including a list of twenty-six names and addresses, turned up in our dual-purpose mail/milk box. Two and a half months later a second letter arrived with thirty-two names and addresses. I didn't even have to ask for it. They were so organized they kept my letter on file and sent me an update. This second list has been misplaced, but I know I must have used it because three people on it responded to my requests.

```
        ADDRESSES OF LIVING MEMBERS OF THE NATIONAL BASEBALL HALL OF FAME
                            As of June 1, 1954

                                                          BIRTHDAYS

 Fred Clarke, Little Pirate Ranch, Winfield, Kansas.      10/ 3/1872

 Tyrus Raymond Cobb, Box 265, Menlo Park, Calif., Glenbrook, Douglas
                County, Nevada.                          12/18/1886

 Gordon Cochrane, Box 937, Lake Forest, Illinois.         4/ 6/1903

 Thomas H. Connolly, 11 Wilson Street, Natick, Mass.     12/30/1870

 Jay Hanna (Dizzy) Dean, 6607 Norway, Dallas, Texas. Works for Falstaff
                Brewing Corp., 3617 Olive St. St. Louis, Mo.  1/16/1911

 William M. Dickey, 22 Sherrill Heights, Little Rock, Arkansas. c/o N.Y.
                American League Baseball Club. 745 - 5th Ave. N.Y.C.  6/ 6/1907

 Hugh Duffy, Boston Red Sox, 24 Jersey St., Boston, Mass.  11/26/1868

 James Emery Foxx, Dormestown Box 127 Giralda, Coral Gables, Fla.  10/22/1907

 Frank Frisch, 184 Fenimore Rd., New Rochelle, New York.   9/ 9/1898

 Charles Gehringer, 16151 James Couzens Highway, Detroit, Michigan.  5/11/1903

 Clark C. Griffith, Washington Baseball Club, Griffith Stadium, Washington
                                                    D.C.  11/20/1869

 Robert Moses Grove, Lonaconing, Maryland                  3/ 6/1900

 Rogers Hornsby, c/o Edgewater Beach Hotel, Chicago, Ill. or c/o Chicago W.Sox.  4/27/1896

 Carl Hubbell, New York Giants, 100 West 42nd St., New York City.  6/22/1903

 Napoleon Lajoie, 188 Daytona Ave., Holly Hill, Florida.   9/ 5/1875

 Connie Mack, Connie Mack Stadium, Philadelphia, Pa.      12/23/1862

 Melvin Thomas Ott, 18 Farnham Place, New Orleans, La.     3/ 2/1909

 Al. Simmons, 1972 South 15th Place, Milwaukee, Wisconsin.  5/22/1903

 George Harold Sisler, Pittsburgh Baseball Club, Forbes Field, Pittsburgh,Pa.  3/24/1893

 Tristram Speaker, 17303 Invermere Rd. Cleveland, Ohio. Sent received  4/ 4/1888

 William H. Terry, Jacksonville, Florida. c/o Terry Motor Company.  10/30/1898

 Harold J. Traynor, 400 - 5th Ave., Pittsburgh, Pa.       11/11/1899

 Honus Wagner, 605 Beechwood Ave. Carnegie, Pa.            2/24/1874

 Roderick J. Wallace, 608 Maryland Ave., El Segundo, Calif.  11/ 4/1874

 Edward A. Walsh, 40 Harrington St., Meriden, Conn. received  5/19/1882

 Paul Waner, c/o Milwaukee Braves, Milwaukee, Wisconsin.   4/16/1903

 Denton T. Young, Newcomerstown, Ohio.                     3/29/1867
```

It was Keener's letter that taught me a lesson I've long remembered: if you are reasonably intelligent and have something to say, you can reach out to almost anyone, if you're sincere. It also showed me that most decent people would respond to a total stranger. Particularly to a kid who is asking questions that make sense.

In those days it only took a three-cent stamp, well, actually two; if you wanted to have a better chance of someone returning an autograph, it was good to enclose a stamp. It wasn't much different from sending in a stamp to get a Lone Ranger ring or a premium from one of the kid radio shows, except they also needed a box top and a dime.

HUGH DUFFY

An autograph from Joe DiMaggio or Dizzy Dean or anyone else only required a simple purple stamp. I don't know why, but most regular-issue three-cent stamps seemed to be purple in those days, as they had been for at least five decades, and this tiny piece of gummed paper was enough to put you in touch with the greatest players of the past and present, even if you lived in a backwater.

I probably began writing letters to the men on the list at a fiendish pace, rapidly depleting the contents of the small metal box in which my mother kept a supply of one-, two- and three-cent stamps. It was a terribly exciting endeavor and within time, probably four or five months, twenty-three of the thirty-two Hall of Famers responded. Nineteen were from the first list and four of the six scheduled for induction in the summer of 1955. This is a remarkable batting average, particularly when one considers that one of the men on the list was deceased, Hugh Duffy, and another, Honus Wagner, was infirm. My batting average was .718. In 2020 there are nearly eighty living members. You'd have to snare fifty plus of them to have the same average. An email won't work, and a stamp is creeping towards twenty times as much, and these days, who writes letters anyway?

I don't remember anything about the others who didn't respond. My guess is it was my fault; perhaps I simply didn't write to them. Some of the men on the first list don't have lines drawn through their names, which probably indicates I didn't send them a letter. Shame on me. But it is astounding that so many of them replied, and because they did I didn't worry about those who didn't.

It really was that simple, write a nice letter, include a bubblegum card, a picture from a magazine, even a scrap of paper, perhaps all three or more, plus return postage, and autographs would turn up. I sent seven pictures, a Hall of Fame card, and a piece of paper to Frankie Frisch, and they all came back, neatly signed, along with a moving letter and a terrific photograph from his collection. It was simply amazing. And they were real autographs. A couple of people, younger active players, used a rubber stamp, but the old-timers didn't.

I'd been writing to my favorite active players for over a year, always sending the letters to them care of the team for which they played. This had been fairly effective. I don't know what the hit ratio was, probably not as good as sending something to someone's home, but many great players, soon to be great players, and a number of ordinary major leaguers replied. Some of them were already celebrated, or at least destined for greatness, and it was just as much fun to get a picture from Ted Williams as Rogers Hornsby. Some even sent team-issued postcards; the Yankees were the only team that had full color cards, at least the only ones I ever saw.

Almost everyone responded with a card or a slip of paper, something with a signature. I recently looked up a list of living members of the Hall of Fame. There is only one person on the list to whom I even wrote a letter, and it is Al Kaline, and when I wrote to him he was twenty years old and twenty-five years away from induction. Time passes.

In 1955 there was no commerce involved in this, but in 2020, commerce is about all there is. Sure, you see the nice pictures of players signing a ball or something for kids at the stadium, but these are the ones who are fortunate enough to have a box seat, close to the field. For everyone else there are autograph tickets, extra fees for personalized autographs, and even more for a bat or a ball or other kinds of equipment, like a glove or a cap.

Some people just buy things off the internet, from dealers or even at auction houses. There are stores in shopping malls devoted to bubblegum cards and memorabilia; there are stores in Manhattan that sell New York Yankee shirts, hats, balls, and here I'm just guessing, everything but underwear. A few years ago I remember hearing an announcement on the radio for an auction of baseball memorabilia at Sotheby's. Joe DiMaggio's rookie uniform was up for only $600,000. It turns out that was chump change. A Babe Ruth uniform has sold for over $4 million; a baseball signed by Mark McGuire for $3 million; a cigarette card of Honus Wagner for over $1 million; and over a $1 million for a 1952 Topps Mickey Mantle card.

The fees are also steep at memorabilia shows; some current stars charge over one hundred dollars for an autograph. There's a sliding scale, so much for a picture, more for a ball, even more for a bat and so forth. It is even worse on the various Major League Baseball websites, where the cheapest items are fifty dollars or more and team bats and balls go for many thousands. It is not unusual for a baseball, signed by a noted active player, to be sold for as much as $500. The holograms, MLB seals, and "certificates of authenticity" that seem to be necessary these days are probably extra.

It seems as if every piece of memorabilia needs to be "authenticated" these days, spawning a cottage industry for "authenticators," perhaps because so much of the material floating around is counterfeit. People who buy these items that are "authenticated" limited editions and so forth don't seem to understand that if something is created to be a "collectible," it never really will be. The Babe Ruth uniform is scarce; is it worth $4,000,000? Probably not, but perhaps it was the only one on the market when it was sold. I'm also sure he had more than one. Imagine playing 150-plus games in one uniform. Not very likely.

Sixty years ago it took a letter and a postage stamp, and the responses were quick in coming. I still have eight envelopes from those days; Connie Mack came back first, less than two weeks from when I received the Hall of Fame list. Frankie Frisch, Nap Lajoie, and George Sisler turned up the same month, followed by Ed Walsh, Ty Cobb, and Rogers Hornsby in March. There were others around the same time, but I didn't save the envelopes, so I have no way to date them. I'm pretty sure all these items are "authentic," and I don't need some guy with a magnifying glass and a hologram to prove it. Those old-time players didn't have someone on the payroll to sign autographs in 1955. And to finance this adventure, my cash outlay for postage, envelopes, bubblegum cards, and pictures clipped from magazines was probably about twenty-five dollars.

Sometime in April or May, I'd written to almost everyone on the list, and I stopped pursuing old-timers and active players with such determination. When the school semester ended and my first season of high school baseball was over, my family returned to Indiana for the summer, and I didn't find my way to the post office very often, but a lot of autographs turned up that summer, after an August ball game in Cincinnati.

Over the next few years I probably sent out an occasional letter because some items are dated in 1956 or 1957, but as soon as I made the high school team (more on that adventure later), I concentrated more on playing than writing. But for a while many wonderful items turned up in the mail, and on the following pages some of these treasures (to me at least) are reproduced. The twenty-three noted below are from men already in the Hall of Fame in 1954-55; the other eighteen are from players who were active at the time and were elected in later years.

HALL OF FAMERS
AS OF 1954–55

1. Frank "Home Run" Baker (1896–1963)
2. Fred Clarke (1872–1960)
3. Ty Cobb (1896–1961)
4. Mickey Cochrane (1903–1962)
5. Dizzy Dean (1911–1974)
6. Joe DiMaggio (1914–1999)
7. Jimmy Foxx (1907–1967)
8. Frankie Frisch (1898–1973)
9. Charlie Gehringer (1903–1993)
10. Clark Griffith (1869–1955)
11. Moses "Lefty" Grove (1900–1975)
12. Leo "Gabby" Hartnett (1900–1972)
13. Rogers Hornsby (1896–1973)
14. Carl Hubbell (1903–1988)
15. Napoleon Lajoie (1875–1959)
16. Connie Mack (1862–1956)
17. Mel Ott (1909–1958)
18. George Sisler (1893–1973)
19. Tris Speaker (1888–1958)
20. Harold "Pie" Traynor (1899–1972)
21. C. A. "Dazzy" Vance (1891–1961)
22. Ed Walsh (1882–1959)
23. Cy Young (1867–1955)

ACTIVE PLAYERS IN 1954–55

1. Richie Ashburn (1927–1997)
2. Lou Boudreau (1917–2001)
3. Roberto Clemente (1934–1972)
4. Larry Doby (1924–2003)
5. Bob Feller (1918–2010)
6. Al Kaline (1934)
7. Ralph Kiner (1922–2014)
8. Bob Lemon (1920–2000)
9. Al Lopez (1908–2005)
10. Mickey Mantle (1931–1995)
11. Johnny Mize (1913–1993)
12. Stan Musial (1920–2013)
13. Robin Roberts (1926–2010)
14. Phil Rizzuto (1917–2007)
15. Albert "Red" Schoendienst (1923–2018)
16. Enos Slaughter (1916–2002)
17. Ted Williams (1918–2002)
18. Early Wynn (1920–1999)

FRANK "HOME RUN" BAKER

I didn't know much about Frank Baker when I wrote to him in the spring of 1955. He was on the second list that had come in from Sid Keener. This list included the men scheduled for induction that summer, so I had no little card or Hall of Fame plaque for him to sign. All I really knew was he had a nifty nickname and was the man Ty Cobb was supposed to have intentionally spiked during the 1909 World Series. Cobb always said it wasn't intentional and sent me a picture of the play to prove it, but it will always be a matter of dispute.

All I had to send him was a picture I'd cut out of a Syracuse newspaper that appeared when he'd been elected to the Hall of Fame, and a piece of paper. He signed and returned both. The colorful cigarette card was obtained a year or so later, once again for ten cents. It's no better a likeness than the newspaper clipping, but it brightens up the page.

I was to later learn Baker didn't hit many home runs, even though, beginning in 1911, he led the league for four years in a row. And during those four years his output was eleven, ten, twelve, and nine home runs, numbers that players today can put up in a month, but these were enough to win the home run crown all those years ago. He only had ninety-six career home runs, but this was enough for a nickname that stuck.

FRED CLARKE

A fiercely competitive player and manager, Fred Clarke was a star from the very beginning of his career. He was only twenty-two when he joined the Louisville Colonels (then in the National League) in 1894. By the time he was twenty-five, he was the manager, a position he retained when Louisville was merged with the Pittsburgh Pirates. He led Pittsburgh until 1915, twenty-one years of service with what was essentially the same team.

His teams won four National League pennants. For a dozen years, beginning in 1901, they were never out of the first division and over a nine-year run had a winning percentage of .634. Along the way Clarke managed to steal over five hundred bases, compile a .312 lifetime batting average, and hit more triples than almost anyone.

In 1915 Clark was forty-three and a little tired. He wasn't hitting well, and his Pirates had finished in the second division for two consecutive years. He decided it was time to retire to his ranch in Kansas, and I don't know if it was the same one to which I wrote in 1955, but it may have been. I wish I'd saved the return envelope that might have read "Little Pirate Ranch." It was a nifty name, but at nearly six feet, Clarke was hardly a "Little Pirate." He was one of the biggest stars they ever had.

CLARKE, PITTSBURG

F. CLARKE, PITTSBURG

TY COBB

In 1955, when kids (and grownups) argued about who was the finest baseball player of all time, it always came down to Babe Ruth or Ty Cobb. Ruth was clearly the more beloved of the two and, unfortunately, the more tragic as well, dying of throat cancer at the young age of fifty-three. He clearly captured the imagination of a nation, and his sunny smile and exploits helped ease the depression blues for millions of Americans.

Ty Cobb, on the other hand, was a rough-and-tumble kind of guy, ornery, overly aggressive, mean-spirited, and often downright nasty, on field and off. He wasn't looking to win a popularity contest, he was just looking to win, all the time, at any cost, and to put up the best numbers of all time. When he retired in 1928, he owned about every possible lifetime record for hitting, except home runs, and most of the season records as well. In 1955 this was still the case, and sixty-five years later, in 2020, he still holds many records, and is in the top five of almost all.

I had no idea this man, who was so vilified, would be so nice to an aspiring young player, but he was, and this story is recounted elsewhere in this book. But pictured here are all the letters, cards, pictures, and pieces of paper he returned to me during the spring of 1955.

TYRUS RAYMOND COBB, THE GEORGIA PEACH

COBB'S FIRST TEAM was the "Little Potatoes" in his home town of Royston, Ga. He is wistful lad—younger than his teammates—seated at far left.

COBB, DETROIT

as he has held up pretty well. I think you should have mentioned Bob Feller more, as I think he is the best pitcher that has come along in quite a while, if he hadn't gone to war he would be close to 400 wins instead of 300.

I wrote to you about 6 months ago, in Detroit, but it was the wrong Ty Cobb. He wrote me a letter telling me he sent it on to you but I guess it got lost.

I would like to know who your favorite pitcher to hit was, I guess you did equally great against all of them, but who was your favorite to hit and who was your worse pitcher to hit?

I am enclosing two pictures and a piece of paper I wish you would please autograph and return.

Walsh, Plank, Grove, Old Cy Young Many others — lets be right in all this Records

Yours truly,
Harold L. Mealy.

Dear Harold:— 14/2/55

I note the fault you found in my Life stories, not mentioning certain players. I had only 12000 words allotted to me to use, the subject was selected or given to me by "Life" I did not choose, If you were a very careful reader of story before you formed and expressed an opinion, you would have seen & realized — I said Musial & Rizzuto was type and example of both players of moderns who could have played in old timer teams. I had to use only 12000 words, of course Ruse & many others you

you to be right as I was, should have enclosed for convenience an addressed and stamped envelope – I receive an average of 4 requests for autographs alone

Harold L. O'Neal, jr.
219 Kensington Rd.
Syracuse 10, N.Y.

Dear Mr. Cobb,

You have always been one of my favorite ballplayers, oo, my grandfather played with you. His name was Curtis Austin Christian, he did not play with you in the majors, only in Macon, Georgia, where he lived. He was a pitcher and his picture was in "Life" magazine in the article you wrote. It was a picture of the sandlot team you were on in Georgia.

I read every word in that series of "Life" magazine articles, and since I was only 12 it was something. I really got a lot out of it, I guess the main thing was hitting to all fields. It really helped me, now I can do it easily. If I could pick it up I don't see why Ted Williams and some of the others couldn't. Because of hitting to all fields I have yet to be put out playing ball in gym, 7 for 7, 6 singles and 1 double, but I can't get much power unless I just stand and hit away. I agreed with most of the things in your article in "Life". I don't guess you mentioned Rosen or Klizewski because they had not quite hit there prime. I don't think that you gave "Pee Wee" Reese enough credit,

Menlo Park, Calif.

TYRUS R. COBB   3/14/55-

Dear Harold Neal:-

Yours received, my
letter was more to explain, not that I
thought you were criticizing. I do
receive many letters from people who
write and in some they differ or
criticize also. so very few or possibly
all are ignorant of the subject,
there is only one way, that is what
are facts and truth. (I am not
referring to you) the records are
available, yet they dont go to trouble
of getting them and being sure to
be right, you seem to like baseball
I am going to trouble to write you
and give title of a book, rather
small, pocket size that have
a greater part of all players
records, and in any difference of
opinions a person with this book
can win such arguments also I
find this book and records so very
interesting my self and many of
the players I played played with or
against for many years, and yet

57

I have more books of records, yearly
records all leagues, books written
that you might have trouble jumping
over and yet I find this book
my favorite and so easy to refer
to, you write Mr. Johnson
Spink, 2018 Washington ave.,
St Louis, (3) Mo. (thats the sporting
News) ask him price on "Daguerreo
Types" of great baseball stars, get
you one of these and you will
thank me.
You ask me of the book "Busting
Em" I have it saw it the other day
in cleaning out and arranging
books etc. I have looked for it and
cannot locate it, I have far too many
of all kinds of books. your mention
of it being written or printed 1914
well thats too far back to be complete
as I played until 1928.
Now there are many baseball books
written also quite a few thats a disgrace
and not worth the paper and by.
so called writers that are not recognized

by the sports writers, these fellows gather up old false stories, print them in book and add provactive stories of their own, at expense of the player who is a star or records of such - a name - they never write of John Smith, Brown or Jones and the story has to be critical and where the name player is shown up, there has been so many stories printed absolutely a lie and never happened but many read and believe them, these stories are put in books to cause same to sell. Zed Williams today is an example of mistreatment. A creature Gene Schor by name wrote a book and it was gotten out hurriedly to capitalize on all the interest caused by the Life stories I did, this book is scandalous also I never have met or remember seeing Schor even, he had Atlanta Ga. newspaper man Bishler to

do so called research in section
I lived, I knew Bishler and
after Scher's book I had a friend
go to Bishler and ask him was
he responsible for things of Ga.
about me, in book, Bishlers
answer was unprintable, he
cursed Scher, saying he went to
expense of auto travel and lots
of time in my section, submitted
his work which he was to be
paid for, Scher did not use most
of it, it never paid him a dime,
but used Bishlers name in
expressing appreciation which was
for only one reason to add the
dignity of Bishlers name, mind you
I did not go to Bishler not that
he would lie to me, but I to make
sure, had a friend of mine also
of Bishlers go to him.
Scher is one man I would have taken
to court, even conferred with a lawyer
but remember anyone can write a book

or story and if they say for
instance, The Story of Ty
Cobb — (big letters) and then
use very small "by" Gene Schoor,
if Schor is a bum and has
nothing, one cannot do anything
except, publicity which draws
public's attention and curiousity
also increase sales of book
So if you want legitimate books of baseball
then select a legitimate writer
anyone else watch out for that word
by.
Git the book I advised then compare
older players with modern records
yourself.

Sincerely
Ty Cobb

P.S. you can write me but I cannot
answer any more —

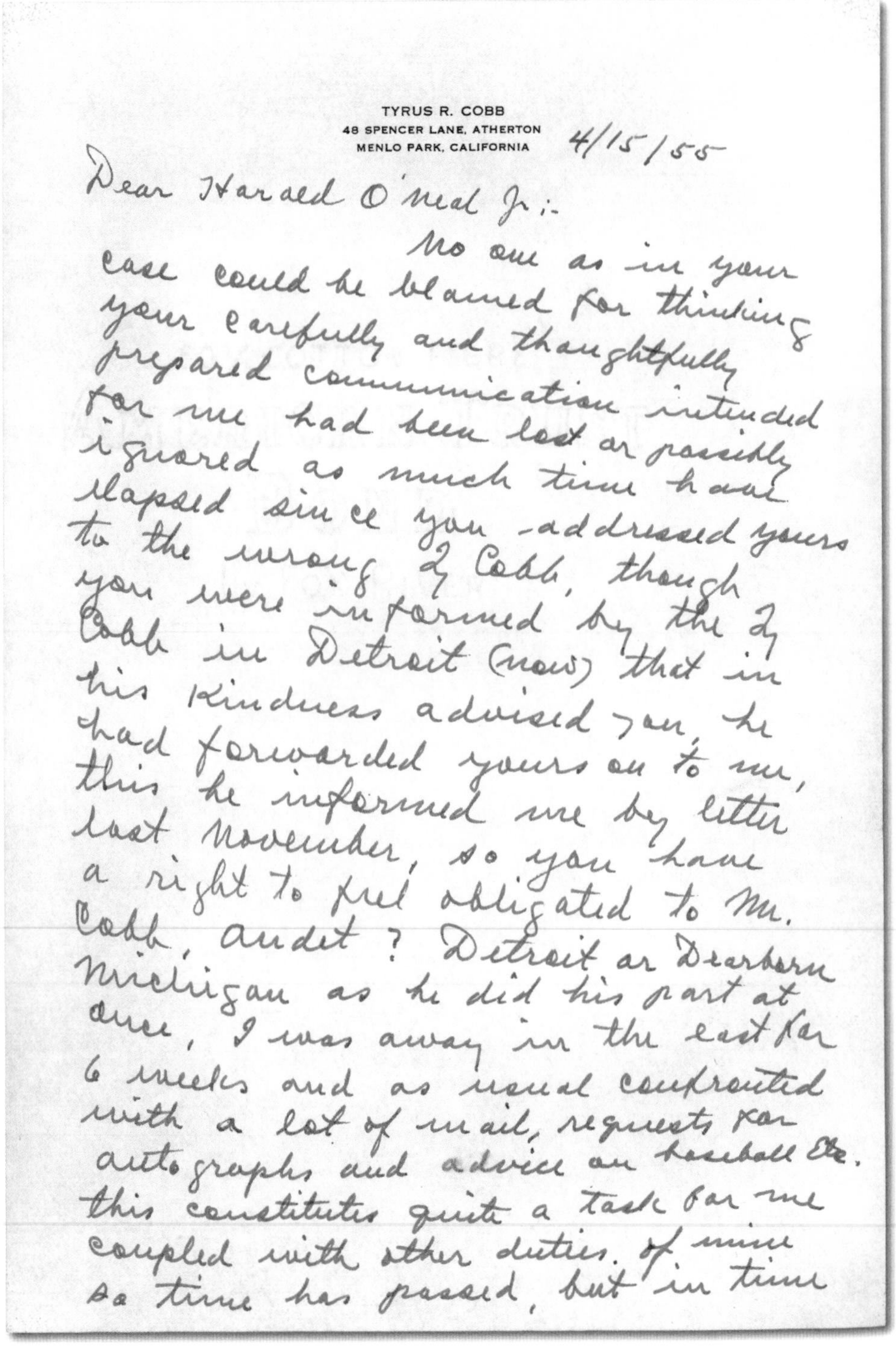

TYRUS R. COBB
48 SPENCER LANE, ATHERTON
MENLO PARK, CALIFORNIA

4/15/55

Dear Harold O'neal Jr.:

No one as in your case could be blamed for thinking your carefully and thoughtfully prepared communication intended for me had been lost or possibly ignored as much time have elapsed since you -addressed yours to the wrong Ty Cobb, though you were informed by the Ty Cobb in Detroit (now) that in his kindness advised you, he had forwarded yours on to me, this he informed me by letter last November, so you have a right to feel obligated to Mr. Cobb, andit? Detroit or Dearborn Michigan as he did his part at once, I was away in the east for 6 weeks and as usual confronted with a lot of mail, requests for autographs and advice on baseball Etc. this constitutes quite a task for me coupled with other duties of mine so time has passed, but in time

I respond or try to and as you
see I have finally gotten to yours.
I always feel honored and complimented
with such requests, though am forced
to say, with the task, I sometime
wish the demands would lessen.
I am returning as you all your
pictures autographed also another
one I add one reason for this is
that so many make demands and
then never have the consideration
to they should and also their duty to
do, in sending the ~~matter~~ material
then the request and take care of return
address, stamps etc. so I commend
you, any boy doing this, his material
and request will never reach
the waste paper basket.
I apologize for my delay as
explained above.
I am,   Sincerely
                         Ty Cobb

P.S. your mention of autographing
pictures and the piece of paper, the
paper must have gotten misplaced
here, I enclose another of mine.
2

63

Harold:- The picture I send is of the so called Baker spiking which I was so unfairly accused of by a drunken sports writer Horace Fogel on some Phila. paper this play was in Detroit so he writes a lurid story really to arouse the fans in Phila so when Detroit came there next would boost the attendance - this has been a practice by the unscrupulous writers, I have always

resented this deeply and the play happened in 1909 - 46 years ago and its still referred to, now very few not more than 6 people have a reprint of this play, so you are one of them, I am making a request of you, if you cannot get the. March - 2nd - 1955 edition of Sporting news (baseball) 2 & 18 washington ave, St. Louis (3) Mo. I request you write them send return postage

. and the cost of paper in stamps, 25 cents tell them why you want it to read Cobbs explanation of Baker spiking, you will no doubt have your stamps returned and will receive this. edition, do not mention I asked you to do this. you will understand it all then, also with the picture I send you, will have an unusual souvenir, I think. Write me when and if. you do this, also your opinion
— 2 —

Harold L. O'neil Jr.,
219 Kensington Road,
Syracuse, (20)
N.Y.

The picture of him running with his eyes closed came from a small booklet that is long lost; the picture of him hitting is from an old baseball magazine. The two cigarette cards came from Wirt Gammon half a century ago; each cost but a dime, and the picture of him sliding into third base, guarded by Home Run Baker, was a present from Cobb himself. He said it was one of only six known copies. That sounds nice, but while this is an old photograph, it was not an old print in 1955. This is a copy on 1950s vintage paper. Nonetheless, sending it to me was a wonderful gesture.

DIZZY DEAN

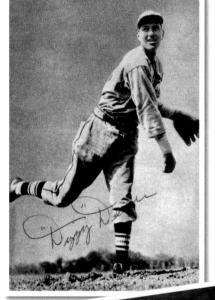

In the early 1950s, probably about 1952 or so, I saw wonderful baseball movie, *The Pride of St. Louis*, and first learned about the exploits of Dizzy Dean. It was a corny movie but a perfect antidote for the B westerns I usually saw in those days. It has been reissued on DVD, but I've never dared look at it again. I'd rather remember that it was terrific at the time, but probably not so good for a grown up in 2020.

Later, I read about Dean in books and magazines and, more importantly, listened to him on the radio, probably beginning in 1953 or 1954. Dean was unlike any announcer I'd ever heard, not that I'd heard many, but who else would sing the "Wabash Cannonball" in the middle of a game? He was a naturally funny guy and not quite as serious as most of the other announcers. That was one of the story lines in *The Pride of St. Louis*. Some people felt his colorful and ungrammatical language would have a negative effect on young listeners like myself, but I'm sure most of us who listened to Dean turned out okay.

I discovered he lived in Dallas, Texas, and when I wrote him, he not only signed the little picture I sent but other things as well, including writing out his return address. He also enclosed a glossy publicity photograph of himself without even being asked. It is filled with his sunny, welcoming smile that was large enough to burst out of the envelope in which he returned the autographs.

The other picture is a mystery. I somehow came up with this picture of Dean and various St. Louis Cardinals about the same time. It is cracked and worn, and I'm not even sure when it was taken, probably in 1947 or 1948. The others in the picture are Stan Musial, Enos Slaughter, and the manager Eddie Dyer.

JOE DIMAGGIO

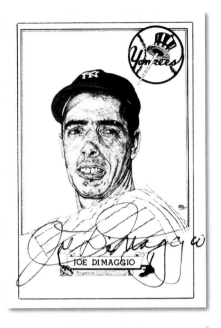

Joe DiMaggio was still a celebrated presence in 1955. He'd retired in 1951, and was elected to the Hall of Fame as soon as he was eligible, probably with almost 100 percent of the votes. He was the only person on my Hall of Fame list who was a youngish but legendary player when I was first learning about baseball. He wasn't an old codger; he was a youngish forty-year-old man who looked like he could still knock the cover off the ball or gracefully run one down in center field.

In 1955 he wasn't the cult figure he was to become in later years, and while he was justly admired for his many accomplishments, the idolatry that encompassed him in the last two decades of his life had not coalesced. In 1955 he didn't charge anything to sign his name on a Hall of Fame card or slips of paper a kid might send him in the mail, and was even kind enough to personalize them. And that's the way I remember him, not as a guy sitting behind a table at a baseball memorabilia show, and that's the way he should be remembered, as a hard-hitting graceful guy who signed an autograph for any kid who asked.

JIMMIE FOXX AND MEL OTT

Jimmie Foxx and Mel Ott were two of the most remarkable power hitters of their era. In many ways their careers were similar; Foxx was primarily active in the American League with Boston and Philadelphia from 1925 to 1945, and Ott was with the New York Giants during the years 1926 to 1948, the last seven as manager. In those years, Foxx hit 534 home runs and led the league in that department four times. Ott hit 511 home runs and led the league six times but didn't have to contend with Lou Gehrig and Babe Ruth. Foxx knocked in 1,921 runs; Ott had 1,861. They also scored about the same: Foxx made it home 1,751 times; Ott was slightly better with 1,859. Each man also led his league in runs batted in, runs, walks, and slugging average at various times. Best of all, they were apparently very nice guys. They had long careers, but both died prematurely, Foxx at fifty-nine and Ott at forty-nine.

FRANKIE FRISCH

I don't remember anything about the magazine article from which I clipped all the pictures of Frankie Frisch that I sent off to be autographed. Sixty years later I'm shocked I was so greedy, even more shocked I got away with it and that he returned a fat envelope full of autographed pictures.

I probably learned from a magazine article that Frisch was known as the "Fordham Flash," and even I knew that this meant he'd gone to college and might be a little better educated than some of his peers. Perhaps this encouraged me to write a more thoughtful, questioning letter, but whatever I wrote was the right thing. Or maybe Frisch was just a nice guy who really cared about kids. I like to think this was the case.

The letter I received from him is remarkable, answering all the questions I posed, offering encouragement, also urging me to pay attention to my studies. He even threw in a picture of his own, the black and white one of him batting, signed *The Old Flash*. I don't remember what I was thinking the day this treasure arrived in the mail, but I'm sure I was astounded.

Feb. 25, 1955

Dear Harold,

It was nice to hear from you, and you will have to excuse my being a little late in answering. The Old Flash has been busy with his Telivision Show, and also doing a little writing.

Now for the questions you asked. Before going into the questions you asked, I hope you will just play ball and enjoy it at your age. You will find that if you listen, you will pick up a great many pointers from the baseball folks that you have contacts with, especially your coaches.

If you can do one of three things, hit, run, or throw, and have a real desire, and have some mentality, and courage, you have a chance to be a big league ball player. At your age, I wish you would just remember this. Get out in the open as much as you can, and participate in the sports you like, and above all don't you forget those studies.

There is one question you asked about hitting. Please remember this - It may be alright to copy sombody els's style of hitting, but in the long run you will find you will be better off if you acquire your own natural comfortable stance, and above all, be sure and have good tools. Don's forget when you walk up to the plate, be sure you have a bat that feels comfortable in your hands. You speak of speed. You don't have to be the fastest man in the world to be a good base runner. A fellow that gets a good jump can do a great job in base stealing.

So now Harold possibly I havn't answered all your questions the way you wanted them, but you know when you speak of records, you can find the Old Flash's records in any of the baseball books. Now that the good old baseball weather is coming around, I hope to hear where you will be leading your team in hitting.

Good luck to you, and be a good boy.

The Old Flash

Frank Frisch

When I reread the letter in 2020, I'm still astounded. Look at the values he stresses: real desire, "some mentality," and courage. Or suggesting to *get out in the open as much as possible and participate in sports you like*. And if this isn't enough, *now that the good old baseball weather is coming around, I hope to hear where you will be leading your team in hitting. Good luck to you and be a good boy.* Still sound advice, but I'm afraid these aren't the values imparted by some of today's most celebrated athletes.

The switch-hitting Frisch was on a pennant winning team eight times with the St. Louis Cardinals and New York Giants. He was a fine hitter, often the league leader in stolen bases, and a record-holding second baseman. He managed the St. Louis Cardinals when they were known as the Gas House Gang and in the 1940s managed the Pittsburgh Pirates and Chicago Cubs.

FRANK FRISCH

CHARLES GEHRINGER

Known as "The Mechanical Man," Charlie Gehringer seems to have done everything precisely by the book, all the way from baseball and penmanship to leading an exemplary and very long life. For fifteen years, between 1926 and 1940, he never hit higher than .371 or lower than .306, winding up with a lifetime average of .320 over nineteen seasons. Along the way, he led the league at one time or another in batting average, hits, doubles, triples, runs, stolen bases, and at the end of his career, pinch hits. His statistics in the field at second base are even more impressive, frequently leading the league in fielding percentage, assists, and put outs. He never associated with any team other than the Detroit Tigers, where, after his playing days, he served as both general manager and vice president for almost a decade. In the late 1960s he was voted the greatest living second baseman.

It would appear his signature was equally mechanical, but my feeling is he signed all the things I sent in his direction and didn't have to resort to a machine or rubber stamp to ensure consistency.

"CHARLEY" GEHRINGER

CHARLES L. GEHRINGER
SECOND BASEMAN WITH DETROIT A.L. FROM
1925 THROUGH 1941 AND COACH IN 1942.
COMPILED LIFETIME BATTING AVERAGE
OF .321 IN 2323 GAMES, COLLECTED 2839
HITS. NAMED MOST VALUABLE PLAYER IN
A.L. IN 1937. BATTED .321 IN WORLD SERIES
COMPETITION AND HAD A .500 AVERAGE
FOR SIX ALL-STAR GAMES.

NATIONAL BASEBALL HALL OF FAME AND MUSEUM
Cooperstown, New York

CLARK GRIFFITH

Clark Griffith was an outstanding pitcher, manager, and club owner, sometimes doing two of these chores at the same time. As a pitcher he had a fine record, winning a total of 240 games during the years 1891 through 1914, including twenty or more six years in a row, 1894-1899. As a manager for four different teams between the years 1901 and 1920, he was in the first division more often than not. He was a player-manager for fourteen of those seasons.

In 1912 he became the manager of the perennial second division Washington Senators and eventually the owner of the franchise, making him, along with Connie

GRIFFITH, CINCINNATI

OF THE
CINCINNATI NATIONALS

GRIFFITH, CINCINNATI

Mack, the only person in Major League Baseball to be a successful player, manager, and owner. Throw in the fact that he was also a player-manager, which Mack was not, and you have an altogether unique individual. From a selfish standpoint, my 1955 letter arrived just in time; he died a few months later in October. I'm amazed he found time to respond to me, but things were different then.

CLARK GRIFFITH

LEFTY GROVE AND DAZZY VANCE

The careers of Dazzy Vance and Lefty Grove overlapped; Vance was primarily active in the National League from 1922 through 1935, and Grove pitched in the American League during the years 1925 through 1941. Each man was a dominating strikeout pitcher, leading their respective leagues seven or eight years in a row, 1922–1928 (Vance) and 1925–1931 (Grove). In four of those years, 1925 through 1928, they overlapped.

An unusual Hall of Famer, Dazzy Vance spent almost as many years in the minor leagues as he did in the majors, and was over thirty years old when he completed his first full season with Brooklyn in 1922. For the better part of the next ten years he was one of the dominant pitchers in the National League, averaging seventeen wins a season during his years with the Dodgers. At various times he also led the league in wins, complete games, shutouts, and earned run average. One wonders what he might have done had his arm not been injured for so many years when he was in his twenties.

Lefty Grove had a more conventional career and, in most ways, a better one. Not only did he frequently lead the league in strikeouts, but he also led the league in earned run average nine times, winning percentage four, and led the league in victories four times. In 1931 he had one of the most spectacular seasons ever recorded by a modern pitcher, winning thirty-one games and only losing four, while leading the league in half a dozen categories. He won three hundred games in his remarkable seventeen-year career. I read somewhere he was known for his bad temper, but by the time I wrote to him in 1955, he'd mellowed and returned my card and piece of paper.

CLARENCE A. "DAZZY" VANCE

ROBERT MOSES GROVE
PHILADELPHIA A.L. 1925 · 1933
BOSTON A.L. 1934 · 1941
WINNER OF 300 GAMES IN THE MAJORS
OVER A SPAN OF 17 YEARS. LED A.L. IN
STRIKEOUTS SEVEN CONSECUTIVE SEASONS.
WON 20 OR MORE GAMES EIGHT SEASONS.
IN 1931, WHILE WINNING 31 GAMES AND
LOSING FOUR, COMPILED A WINNING STREAK
OF 16 STRAIGHT. WON 79 GAMES FOR THE
THREE TIME PENNANT WINNING
ATHLETICS TEAM OF 1929-30-31.

NATIONAL BASEBALL HALL OF FAME AND MUSEUM
Cooperstown, New York

GABBY HARTNETT AND MICKEY COCHRANE

Gabby Hartnett was the premier catcher/manager in the National League for twenty years between 1922 and 1941; Mickey Cochrane was an equally outstanding catcher/manager in the American League for fourteen years, 1925 through 1938. Each was voted to the All-Star team on multiple occasions and won most valuable player awards. During their playing career, neither was ever in first place in any offensive category, though each regularly won defensive awards. Despite never winning a batting championship, Cochran's lifetime average is the best of any major league catcher, and Hartnett is generally recognized as the finest National League catcher prior to the emergence of Johnny Bench.

LEO "GABBY" HARTNETT

ROGERS HORNSBY

ROGERS HORNSBY

My first introduction to Rogers Hornsby was in a 1952 movie, *The Winning Team*, a standard Hollywood biopic about the legendary pitcher, Grover Alexander. Ronald Reagan played Alexander, and Frank Lovejoy was Hornsby. Later, after I saw a picture of Hornsby, I realized the casting was very good.

In 1955, Hornsby was nearly sixty and between assignments. His last significant job in baseball had been in 1952, as manager of the usually hapless St. Louis Browns. It was to be his last managerial position, and even though it was just across town, the lowly Browns never challenged the St. Louis Cardinals, where Hornsby had made his name as possibly the finest National League hitter of all time. Hornsby was second only to Ty Cobb in career batting average and still holds the modern-day record for a single season batting average, .424 in 1924.

Honor to Admired Opponent

I was puzzled that someone would be living full time at a hotel, but I sent the cards and paper to the hotel in Chicago listed as his address on the Hall of Fame address sheet. It worked; everything came back signed, and I was thrilled. The yellowing picture is from an old newspaper I found in the attic of the Civil War-era house a friend of the family bought in southern Indiana in the early 1950s. Interestingly enough, the paper featured a pictorial article about the 1926 World Series, and the picture of Grover Alexander didn't look anything like Ronald Reagan.

CARL HUBBELL

A quiet, taciturn man, Carl Hubbell built his career on one of the most difficult pitches, the screwball. Apparently he threw it so frequently, for so many years, that his left arm was permanently turned outward. I was always fond of anyone who threw this pitch; I'd toyed with it, and while I never really mastered the rarely used pitch, I was able to use it on occasion after I hurt my arm in my senior year. For some reason, my arm throbbed when I tried to throw a curve, but there was no problem if I twisted it the other way and attempted a screwball.

Carl Hubbell had no such problems. He was the mainstay of the New York Giants pitching staff for a decade and a half, until he ran out of gas at the age of forty in 1943. His best years were in the mid-1930s, particularly in 1936 and 1937, when he won twenty-four consecutive games. He was equally remarkable in 1933, when he led the league in wins, earned run averages, innings pitched, and saves. He helped propel the Giants to pennants in each of those years, and when his playing days ended, remained with the club in various capacities until 1977.

CARL HUBBELL
NEW YORK N.L. 1928-1943
HAILED FOR IMPRESSIVE PERFORMANCE IN
1934 ALL-STAR GAME WHEN HE STRUCK OUT
RUTH, GEHRIG, FOXX, SIMMONS AND CRONIN
IN SUCCESSION. NICKNAMED GIANTS'
MEAL-TICKET. WON 253 GAMES IN MAJORS,
SCORING 16 STRAIGHT IN 1936. COMPILED
STREAK OF 46⅓ SCORELESS INNINGS IN
1933. HOLDER OF MANY RECORDS.

NATIONAL BASEBALL HALL OF FAME AND MUSEUM.
COOPERSTOWN. NEW YORK

NAPOLEON LAJOIE

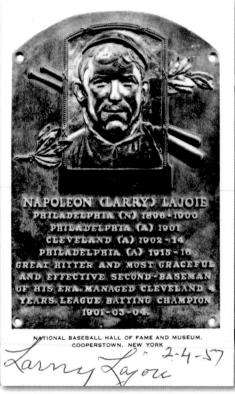

LAJOIE, CLEVELAND

I still have the tattered December 1952 issue of the long-forgotten magazine, *Inside Baseball*, a fine publication that appeared in that year. I don't know if it survived past that year; the issue I have is number five and who knows if there was a number six. But my issue contained an article by a man named John McCallum entitled "Nap Lajoie—The Fabulous Frenchman."

This wasn't the first time I'd ever heard of Lajoie. But it was in this article that I discovered he was a remarkably resilient second baseman, lasting twenty-one seasons. He was a Triple Crown winner in 1901, hitting .422, still an American League record, wound up with a lifetime average of .338, and frequently led the league in hits and doubles. If that wasn't enough, he may well have been the best fielding second baseman of his day. He was elected to the Hall of Fame in 1937, just behind the original group of Cobb, Johnson, Ruth, Mathewson, and Wagner.

The first time I read about him was in *Big-Time Baseball*, a 1950 publication that told fanciful stories about noted stars of the past and present. The story they told about Lajoie, *The Second Base Smoothie*, involved the American League making a movie in 1934 about how to play baseball. The fifty-nine-year-old Lajoie was selected to illustrate the perfect hitting technique. He'd been retired for years but still had a flawless swing. This is a movie I'd love to see.

The *Inside Baseball* article said Lajoie lived in Daytona Beach, Florida, and perhaps he did; he died in that city in 1959, but the Hall of Fame listed him in Holly Hill, Florida, and that's where I sent the letter in February 1955. The photograph is from the old magazine article. I must've written him again in February 1957, because that's when he signed and dated the Hall of Fame plaque.

CONNIE MACK

The oldest member of the Hall of Fame to whom I wrote was Connie Mack. He was ninety-two at the time, and I'm not sure, but I probably didn't hold out much hope of getting an autograph. But it was worth a try; Connie Mack had been part of Major League Baseball from the beginning, or almost the beginning. Major League Baseball was only a decade old when he made his debut with Washington in 1886. And it turned out my six cents and time were well-spent.

Mack began his career as a manager with Pittsburgh in 1894, but it was his relationship with the Philadelphia Athletics by which he is judged. He was the manager for fifty straight seasons, 1901 to 1950, and during that time his teams not only won 3,776 ballgames but seven American League pennants as well.

As luck would have it, Mack's son, Roy Mack, had a supply of cards his father had signed the year before, when he was stronger, and he sent one along to me. Some years later I traded something—I don't remember what—for a ball he'd signed in 1947. Roy Mack's letter to me is dated February 18, 1955. Connie Mack died less than a year later on February 8, 1956.

GEORGE SISLER

GEORGE SISLER

I managed to track down George Sisler when he was associated with the Pittsburgh Pirates and his old friend, the legendary Branch Rickey. Sisler was a special hitting instructor. This is not surprising since he was one of the finest batsmen of his day; his 257 hits in 1920 was the benchmark, until it was surpassed by Ichiro Suzuki in 2004 (262). But to put things in perspective, in addition to the .407 batting average he had 399 total bases, with forty-nine doubles, eighteen triples, and nineteen home runs, and he drove in 122 runs and stole forty-two bases. Suzuki also played seven more games.

Two years later Sisler led the league once again, hitting .420, the third best in the twentieth century. That year he also led the league in runs, hits, triples, and stolen bases. The only thing that slowed him down was illness that caused him to have double vision, and even though his eyes never fully recovered, he still managed to have a lifetime batting average of .340.

TRIS SPEAKER

His Hall of Fame plaque states emphatically that Tris Speaker was the finest centerfielder of his day. In later years, the same could have been said of Joe DiMaggio, and it is interesting to me that I have their signatures together on an old ball. I never saw either player in action, but my guess is DiMaggio may have been more graceful, though Speaker covered a bit more ground because he played so close to the infield.

Admittedly, Speaker played in a different era, when people didn't hit the ball nearly as far as they do in 2020, but it still seems remarkable that he is still the all-time leader in double plays and assists. I remember reading somewhere that he even had a few unassisted double plays to his credit, a remarkable feat for an outfielder. I wonder if there will be a single double play generated by an outfielder this season.

Speaker was even better with his bat and over a twenty-two-year career is in the lifetime top ten in average, hits, doubles (first), triples, runs, extra-base hits, and total bases. He was also a successful player-manager during the years 1919–1926 and remained in baseball in various capacities into the 1950s, ending his career with the Cleveland Indians.

TRIS SPEAKER

SPEAKER, BOSTON AMER.

TRISTRAM E. (TRIS) SPEAKER
BOSTON (A) 1909-16
CLEVELAND (A) 1916-26
WASHINGTON (A) 1927
PHILADELPHIA (A) 1928
GREATEST CENTREFIELDER OF HIS
DAY. LIFETIME MAJOR LEAGUE BATTING
AVERAGE OF .344 MANAGER IN 1920
WHEN CLEVELAND WON ITS FIRST
PENNANT AND WORLD CHAMPIONSHIP.

NATIONAL BASEBALL HALL OF FAME AND MUSEUM
Cooperstown, New York

PIE TRAYNOR

"PIE" TRAYNOR

When he retired from active play in 1937, Pie Traynor was generally considered to be the finest third baseman in baseball history. He was not a fearsome hitter; in fact, he only led the league a single time in any offensive category, triples in 1923 (nineteen), but he was remarkably reliable over seventeen years and wound up with a lifetime batting average of .320 and 2,416 hits. Traynor spent his entire career with the Pittsburgh Pirates and is among the team leaders in every offensive category except home runs. He served as manager or player-manager for his final six seasons. In 1969 he was selected as the all-time third baseman for baseball's centennial year.

HAROLD J. (PIE) TRAYNOR
RATED AMONG THE GREAT THIRD BASEMEN
OF ALL TIME, BECAME A REGULAR WITH
THE PITTSBURGH N.L. TEAM IN 1922 AND
CONTINUED AS A PLAYER UNTIL CONCLUSION
OF 1937 SEASON. MANAGED THE PIRATES
FROM JUNE, 1934, THROUGH SEPT. 1939. HOLDS
SEVERAL FIELDING RECORDS AND COMPILED
A LIFETIME BATTING MARK OF .320. ONE OF
FEW PLAYERS EVER TO MAKE 200 OR MORE
HITS DURING A SEASON, COLLECTING
208 IN 1923.

NATIONAL BASEBALL HALL OF FAME AND MUSEUM
Cooperstown, New York

ED WALSH

WALSH, CHICAGO AMER.

Ed Walsh was the only "official" spitball pitcher on my Hall of Fame list. He was a remarkable turn-of-the-century player, one who didn't last too many years but who was remarkably effective during his best seasons. He didn't even win two hundred games in his fourteen seasons, but he played for a weak hitting team that produced few runs. I learned there were two things that set him apart from other pitchers: he once won forty games in a season, and he had the lowest lifetime earned run average of any pitcher, 1.82.

His record ERA is a remarkable number. In today's world, or in the world of 1955, the guy who leads the league in that department is usually on the north side of 2.00, often way north of that number. In the 2010s there are only three active pitchers who have a lifetime in the upper 2.00s, and most are above 3.00. Occasionally a pitcher breaks 2.00; in fact, Billy Pierce did in 1955 with 1.97, but that was only one year and his lifetime number is 3.27.

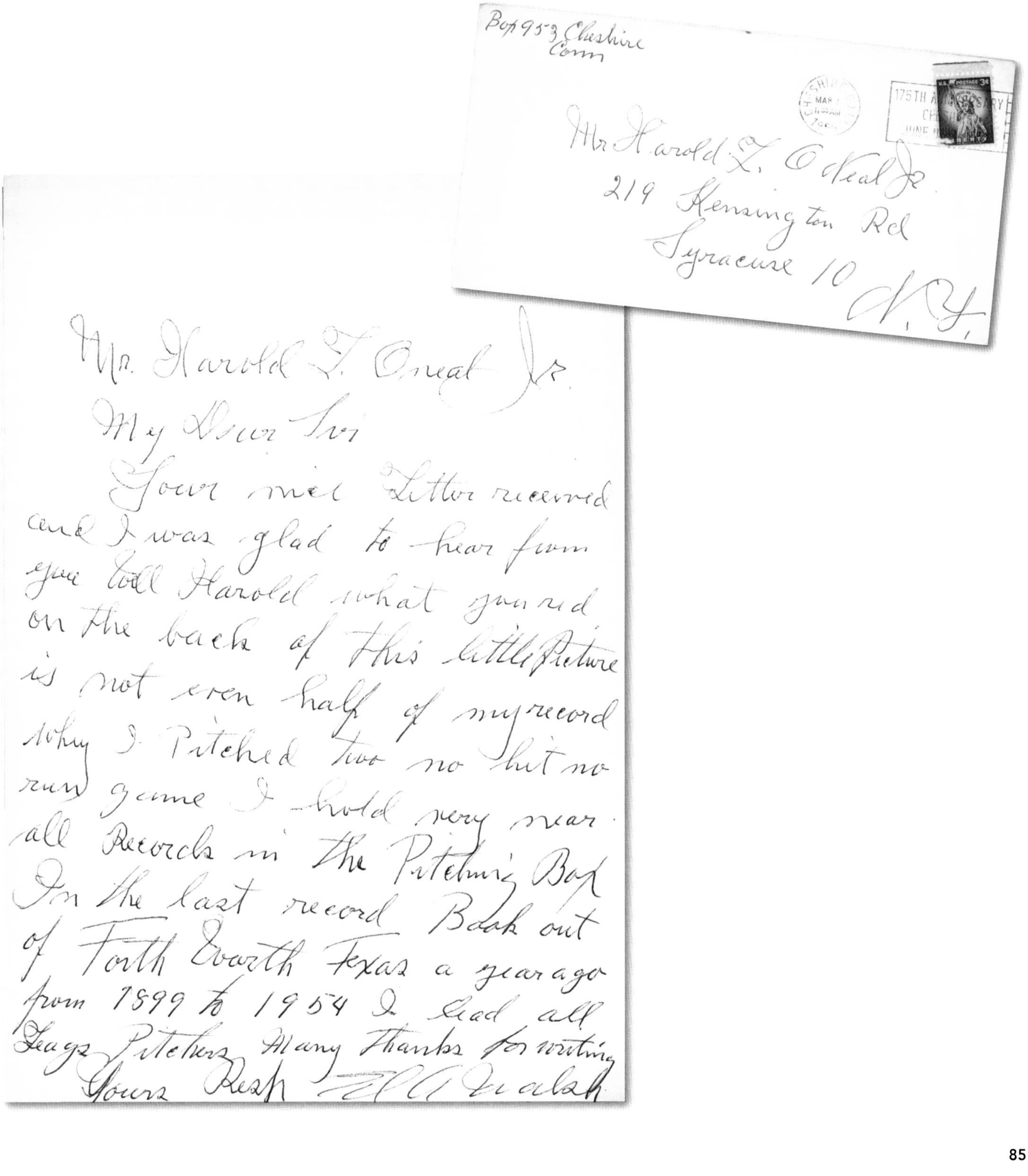

Box 953 Cheshire
Conn

Mr. Harold T. O'Neal Jr.
219 Kensington Rd
Syracuse 10
N.Y.

Mr. Harold T. Oneal Jr.

My Dear Sir

Your nice Letter received and I was glad to hear from you tell Harold what you read on the back of this little Picture is not even half of my record why I Pitched two no hit no run game I hold very near all Records in the Pitching Box In the last record Book out of Forth Worth Texas a year ago from 1899 to 1954 I lead all Leags Pitchers Many Thanks for writing

Yours Resp Ed A Walsh

Walsh put up incredible numbers, playing for a team that apparently could barely hit the ball out of the infield. In 1910, for example, he won eighteen games, lost twenty, and had an ERA of 1.27, an incredibly low number but not good enough to keep him from losing more games than any other pitcher in that year. In modern times Dwight Gooden came closest with a 1.53 ERA in 1985 but never was near that number in subsequent years. Gooden had twenty-four wins in his best year and only four losses. Times change.

The letter Walsh sent to me seems to be written with care, and the handwriting looked much like my grandfather's. It is courtly and proper, full of flourish, a product of the kind of penmanship that was taught to all children in the late 1800s. Like the other letters from Cobb and Frisch, he talks about records; he was very proud of what he'd accomplished and was probably happy to be remembered and contacted by a fourteen-year-old aspiring player.

ED WALSH

CY YOUNG

Somehow, I found out where Cy Young lived before Sid Keener sent me the Hall of Fame list, and I wrote to him in the summer of 1954. I could barely believe he won 511 games in his twenty-two-year career. He won over thirty games in five different seasons and over twenty in fourteen consecutive years, 1891–1904. In 1954 there were only a few active pitchers who had even won a couple of hundred, and no one had won thirty in one season since Dizzy Dean won thirty in 1934. Ultimately, two pitchers active in 1954 would reach 300 wins: Early Wynn with 300 and Warren Spahn with an astounding 363, but no one has even come close to Young's record. Fourteen years later, Denny McLain won thirty-one games in 1968 but had an abbreviated career and was a disappointment professionally and personally.

I clipped the photograph from a baseball magazine and enclosed it with a slip of paper along with a return envelope. Both came back on August 31, 1954. There was a bonus signature because the mailing sticker was also signed. The two cigarette cards were obtained a year or so later from my pen pal with old cards for sale, Wirt Gammon, for twenty cents.

Cy Young was eighty-seven when he signed this picture for me. He died the next year on November 4, 1955. I was lucky to have found his address in 1954.

YOUNG, CLEVELAND

YOUNG, CLEVELAND

LOU BOUDREAU AND AL LOPEZ

Between the years 1942 and 1956, the Cleveland Indians were blessed with back-to-back Hall of Fame managers. I don't know for sure, but this may have been one of the few times this ever happened. Lou Boudreau, a player-manager, was at the helm from 1942 to 1950, and Al Lopez, whose playing days were long behind him, was in charge from 1951 through 1956. Each man managed one league pennant—Boudreau in 1948, Lopez in 1954. Boudreau led his team to a World Series victory; Lopez, with what was probably a better team, was skunked in 1954 by the New York Giants in four games. Yet Lopez's Cleveland Indians never finished lower than second place during the six years he was in charge.

Lopez actually finished his playing career with Cleveland in 1947, playing under Boudreau's tutelage. This was his introduction to the American League, where he spent the rest of his career as a coach or manager until 1969. Boudreau managed three different teams after his years with Cleveland. His last was with the Chicago Cubs in 1960. He then retired to the Cubs broadcast booth, where he remained for many years.

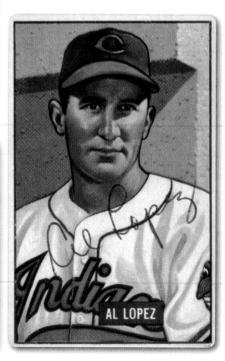

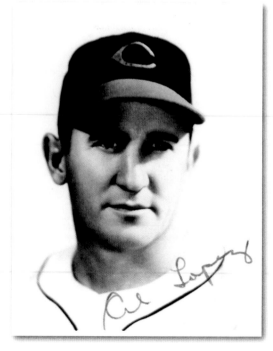

ROBERTO CLEMENTE
AND AL KALINE

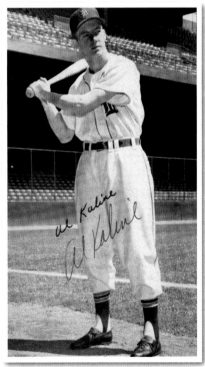

By today's standards, Roberto Clemente and Al Kaline were unique. Clemente spent his entire eighteen-year career with Pittsburgh, 1955 through 1972; Al Kaline spent his twenty-two-year career with Detroit, 1953 through 1974. People just don't do that any longer, particularly men with the skills possessed by these two outfielders, each of whom won multiple Golden Glove awards.

Clemente hit the ball more regularly; he led the league in batting average four times, but Kaline hit it a little harder. Kaline had 399 home runs and Clemente had 240. Each man was a superior hitter: Kaline ended his career with 3,007 hits, and Clemente managed an even 3,000, but his playing days were cut short when he died in an airplane crash while delivering relief supplies to earthquake-devastated Nicaragua.

Al Kaline went from being the face of the Tigers to its voice as well. When he retired from active play in 1974, he went upstairs to the broadcasting booth and remained there for many years. We will never know what the future would have held for Clemente, but he surely had some remarkable days in front of him.

LARRY DOBY, BOB LEMON, AND EARLY WYNN

In the late 1940s and early 1950s, the Cleveland Indians were blessed with an array of stars, many of whom would be elected and enshrined in the Hall of Fame. The team was unusually good; they won the pennant in 1948 and 1954, but were usually also-ran to the New York Yankees. For some reason, they were my favorite team, so I wrote more letters to Cleveland players than to players on any other team.

Larry Doby is distinctive for many reasons: he was the first African American player in the American League, joining Cleveland in the same year Jackie Robinson broke the color barrier in Brooklyn, but Doby did it a few months later, on July 5, in Cleveland. Robinson hit for average and stole bases; Doby hit home runs and knocked them in. At various times in his thirteen-year career he led the league in home runs, runs, and runs batted in.

Bob Lemon was an outstanding pitcher for fifteen years. He won twenty games or more seven times, pitched ten shutouts in 1948, led the league in various seasons in wins, game started, complete games, shutouts, innings pitched, and strikeouts. In 1950 he led the league in six different categories. After his active playing years, he managed the Kansas City Royals, the Chicago White Sox, and the New York Yankees and was voted manager of the year in 1971 and 1977. The only possible blemish on an otherwise spectacular career occurred in 1994 when he consented to my request that he write the liner notes for a CD I released featuring his old friend, Flip Phillips.

Early Wynn was a remarkably durable pitcher, working twenty-three seasons in the American League with Washington, Cleveland, and Chicago. His best years were with Cleveland, where he posted 178 of his 300 wins. He was, reportedly, a rough, intimidating pitcher. The numbers he put up and the length of his career would indicate this, but he signed everything I sent in his direction, so he must have had a soft spot somewhere. He led the league in many categories on multiple occasions: wins, ERA, complete games, strikeouts, innings pitched, and shutouts. When he retired, his twenty-three seasons on the mound was the longest service of any pitcher.

HANK GREENBERG AND RALPH KINER

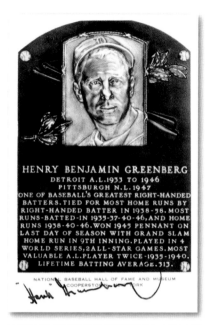

Hank Greenberg and Ralph Kiner were among the most fearsome sluggers in their respective leagues and had much in common, on and off the playing field. Greenberg was a decade older and spent his entire career with Detroit, except for his final season. In 1947 Detroit sold Greenberg to Pittsburgh, where he played one year. But that same year, Ralph Kiner had a simply spectacular season with the same team. He was in his second season with Pittsburgh, hit fifty-one home runs, and also led the league in slugging average and home run percentage. He was to lead the league in home runs for the next five seasons.

In 1947, the only season they played together, the two sluggers were roommates on the road and together managed seventy-six home runs. By 1955, when Kiner's career was winding down because of a bad back, Greenberg was the general manager of the Cleveland Indians and brought his roommate to that team for a final season. Greenberg remained as an executive in baseball until 1963; Kiner became the voice of the New York Mets in 1962 and kept the job for over forty years.

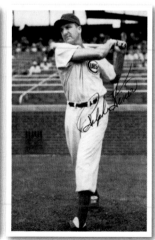

MICKEY MANTLE
AND PHIL RIZZUTO

MICKEY MANTLE
outfielder NEW YORK YANKEES

In the 1950s, I don't think any young player captured the public's imagination as did Mickey Mantle, and half a century later, his legendary status seems secure. He could hit the ball into the farthest reaches of Yankee stadium from either side of the plate and did so regularly. His teammate, Phil Rizzuto, was fourteen years older, had been a Yankee for a decade when Mantle arrived on the scene, and was his exact opposite. He was a tiny hustling shortstop who was not known for his slugging prowess, but still managed to win the most valuable player award in 1950, an award Mantle won in 1956, 1957, and 1962.

When Rizzuto retired in 1956, he changed his clothes and went upstairs to the Yankees broadcast booth where he remained for forty years, retiring in 1996 with nearly seventy years with the New York Yankee organization. After Mantle's playing days were over, he found his way into the broadcast booth for a single season in 1969.

I never saw Rizzuto in a game except on television, but in 1966 I did get to see Mantle in Washington, DC. He was having a hard time; my guess is his legs were bandaged from top to bottom. He only had ninety-six hits that year, but I saw two of them. I was sitting on the first base side and remember it was obvious how hard he was straining just to run to first base. But somehow he managed, that day and on many others during his incredible eighteen-year career. I'm still amazed by the autograph he returned to me in 1955; it was on the back of the letter I wrote to him.

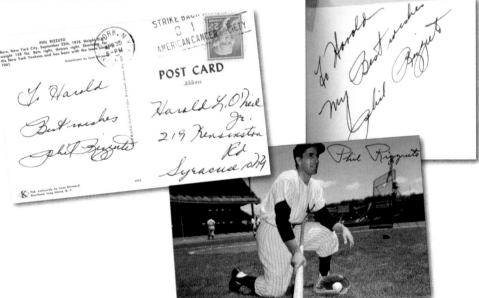

JOHNNY MIZE AND ENOS SLAUGHTER

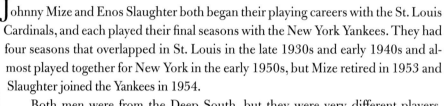

Johnny Mize and Enos Slaughter both began their playing careers with the St. Louis Cardinals, and each played their final seasons with the New York Yankees. They had four seasons that overlapped in St. Louis in the late 1930s and early 1940s and almost played together for New York in the early 1950s, but Mize retired in 1953 and Slaughter joined the Yankees in 1954.

Both men were from the Deep South, but they were very different players. Mize was slow and lumbering and was a slugger, leading the league in home runs four times and, in eight seasons, had over one hundred runs batted in. Slaughter was a hustler who could beat you a dozen different ways. At one time or another he led the league in hits, doubles, triples, and runs batted in, and in a nineteen-year career he had a .300 lifetime batting average. In fifteen seasons, Mize had a career average of .312, and also hit 359 home runs.

Mize was responsible for the first Major League Baseball heroics I can remember. It was in 1952, during the first World Series I ever saw on television. He was almost forty years old and by then was mainly just a pinch hitter. But I still remember seeing him on a tiny black and white screen when he hit three home runs in the series to help lead the New York Yankees to victory.

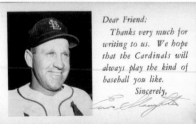

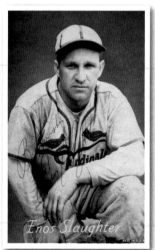

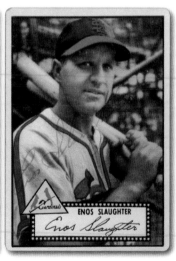

STAN MUSIAL AND RED SCHOENDIENST

In the mid-1950s, the St. Louis Cardinals supplied their players with postcards to send out to their fans. It appears they also gave them rubber stamps to use as substitutes for real autographs. The only rubber-stamped "autographs" I ever received from anyone were from St. Louis Cardinals.

Stan Musial was probably the most consistent hitter of his era and over twenty-three seasons accumulated many, many records. He also had more admiring fans than any of the other stars of the 1940s and 1950s. This was not just because of his ability on the field but also because of his easy-going, friendly demeanor when he was not playing. I never had a baseball card to send to him; all that turned up in my mailbox was the rubber-stamped piece of paper. Maybe he'd run short of postcards that day.

Red Schoendienst was on all sorts of cards, but in those days he rubber-stamped them as well, in red ink. He will forever be associated with St. Louis, both as a player for fifteen seasons and as a manager for thirteen. He was almost as consistent in his play at second base as Musial was as a hitter. He was in three World Series as a player and two as a manager. His Cardinals won the World Series in 1967.

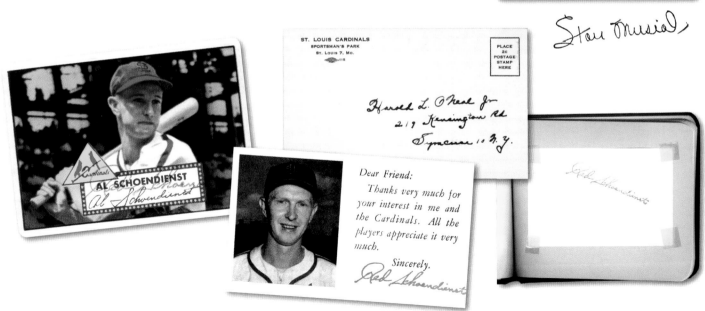

ROBIN ROBERTS AND RICHIE ASHBURN

In 1950 the Philadelphia Athletics finished last in the American League, but across town the Phillies, who hadn't won anything since 1915, managed to morph into the "Whiz Kids" and edge out the Brooklyn Dodgers by two games. The team boasted a number of exceptional players, and a couple were at the beginning of what would become Hall of Fame careers. The two were its premier pitcher, Robin Roberts, and its fleet-footed, solid-hitting outfielder, Richie Ashburn.

Ashburn had a fine fifteen-year career in the National League, ending his playing days with the lowly New York Mets in 1962. Along the way he managed to collect 2,500 hits and nearly 1,200 base on balls, a category in which he led the league four times. In 1958 he won the batting championship and led the league in hits, triples, base on balls, and a few other categories. Robin Roberts lasted a few years longer, a nineteen-year career that produced 286 wins, usually for teams that weren't very good. He led the league in wins for four consecutive years and in half a dozen other categories in multiple years.

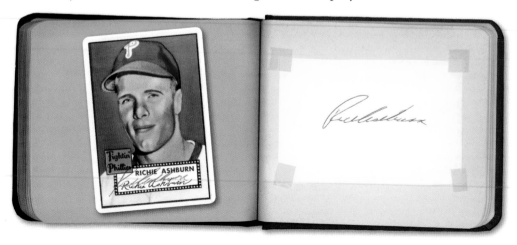

TED WILLIAMS

Ted Williams was simply the finest hitter of the modern era. His lifetime statistics are remarkable and probably would've been unsurpassed if he hadn't missed five full seasons because of World War II and Korea. It is commonplace to talk about Williams hitting .406 in 1941, the last person to reach that plateau, but what is often overlooked is that when he left for Korea in 1952, he was hitting .400 after six games, and when he returned in 1953 he hit .407 in thirty-seven games. He also managed to hit thirteen home runs in this abbreviated season. He had one full .400 season and two abbreviated ones.

At one time or another he led the league in almost every offensive category except hits, because he generally was the league leader in walks. He was first in that category eight times, including six consecutive years. If you combine his hits and walks, he was probably on base more than anyone else throughout his career. It's a pity he missed five seasons, but my guess is he enjoyed flying jets in Korea as much as he enjoyed hitting balls out of Fenway Park.

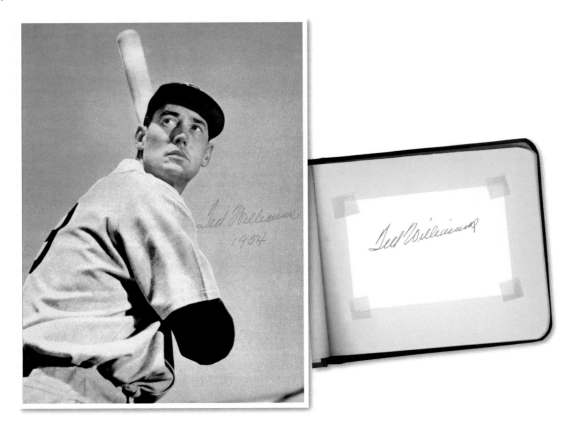

Many sportswriters and some fans found him offensive in some ways. He didn't tolerate fools gladly or criticism from any quarter, but he tolerated me and signed everything I sent in his direction, and he even sent me back a black-and-white picture for good measure. My guess is these are real signatures; in later years, along with Joe DiMaggio, his autograph was one of the most blatantly forged, but in 1955 he wasn't selling them and neither was anyone else. And there weren't any scandals of the sort that occurred after he died in 2002. I found all the terrible maneuvering within his family after his death simply disgusting. This is something best forgotten.

I vividly remember his last game in 1960. I wasn't there; I was sitting on a friend's porch in Syracuse, New York, watching the game on a small black-and-white television. Williams came to bat for what everyone assumed would be his last time. He promptly knocked the ball out of the park. I remember he didn't tip his hat that day and it probably caused some consternation. I looked it up, and a third of his hits were home runs that final year. He could probably have hit even more in subsequent seasons if he didn't want to become the world's finest fisherman.

I also went on the internet, typed in the words "Ted Williams' last time at bat," and found that someone had preserved the moment as a black and white film or kinescope. So I can now go back in time for a minute any time I'd like and watch him hit it again.

THE LAST
UNIFORM

The baseball game Cobb wrote about and actually playing baseball was another matter. It had been two years since I'd played a serious game except with the garage wall, and I needed some inspiration. Letters, autographs, and occasional conversations from and with Ty Cobb and other players, old and new, helped a lot but this was not *playing the game*. The foolish ball games in gym class with an extra soft softball didn't count either, no matter how many "hits" I managed to collect. I also knew the gym teacher in February was the baseball coach in April, and he was the guy I had to impress.

Unfortunately I was lousy in the kinds of things normally associated with gym class—jumping over parallel bars, swinging on rings, climbing ropes, and assorted gymnastic nonsense. This was nothing but indoor exercise, as dull to me as the book reports I prepared for English class. But I faced a problem with the gym teacher I didn't face with the grammarian. I didn't care about impressing the English teacher, but I knew that in the next few weeks I had to impress the gym instructor, who was soon to be my hoped-for baseball coach.

Tryouts for the baseball team were scheduled to begin in late March, indoors unfortunately, in the same gymnasium where I regularly fell off the parallel bars. Looking for any advantage, I managed to acquire a new glove for the tryouts and, attempting to cash in on past glories, I selected a Jim Busby model. It proved to be a good choice. Nearly six decades later it still works very well, but is about half the size of the breadbaskets used by many players today. It was a full-size glove in 1955, and I don't think it has shrunk. Maybe they changed the rules when I wasn't looking and gloves on steroids have become legal.

I didn't have much going for me when tryouts began; I was too young, too skinny, needed glasses but didn't know it (and I didn't throw like Ryan Duren, who needed glasses and knew it but made his opponents think he didn't!) and was up against a bunch of kids who'd been playing together for years. On the face of it, the odds of my making the team, even as a mascot, were pretty slim. I gained some confidence when I made the first couple of cuts; the first cut sent the lame and paralyzed to the showers and the marginally coordinated were sent packing soon thereafter.

This left about fifty healthy, eager kids looking to get one of the twenty or so dreary gray uniforms with the name of the school, Nottingham, stitched across the front in blue. They were much worse than those worn by the "Horned Frogs" some years

earlier. A blue cap with a large orange N was also part of the deal for the lucky twenty who were selected for the team.

I needed some kind of miracle. It didn't do me much good to think about my Ty Cobb letters and anything he'd written to me. In fact, I couldn't even tell anyone about them. I was certain I'd be the object of scorn and ridicule from my classmates if they knew about my correspondence. Imagine what they'd think—look at this new kid, he's fourteen years old and still writing fan letters to some old baseball player. No, thinking about a letter from Cobb, Frisch, or anyone else was not the answer, but maybe taking a lesson from the young Ty Cobb could make a difference or perhaps just imagining the headlong way in which he wrote.

I remembered in the *Life* articles he said he didn't start out with great skills, that he simply hustled and was very determined to make good. He said he never missed a chance to practice or to play a game. Maybe ambition and hustle could make up for lack of skill and youth, but I was certain it would make no difference in that lousy gymnasium, working out on wooden floors as we waited for the snow to melt and the weather to warm enough to go outdoors. Somehow, I managed to hang on.

We finally moved out of the gymnasium but, unhappily, onto a gravel-littered asphalt parking lot in front of the school. This was better than being inside, but not much. It was fine for hitting and catching anything in the air, but I wasn't trying to sell either of those talents. I wanted to make the team as a pitcher, and we had to use terrible rubber-coated baseballs because a normal ball would have been cut to ribbons by the asphalt and loose gravel. The rubber balls were also ruined pretty quickly, but the reality was that while these phony balls could be thrown fairly hard they had no seams, just artificial ridges to grip for an attempted curve, screwball, or knuckler.

My talent was sufficiently modest that I wanted to be able to show off whatever I could, but these balls made it all but impossible. All I could do was pretend a hitter was a sketched figure on the garage wall and throw as hard and accurately as possible, which I did whenever asked. I threw that rubber baseball like my life depended on it, and in a small way it did, because if I didn't make the team it would mean yet another year of no organized baseball, which in my mind meant that my never very spectacular "career" would be over forever and I would be shunned by all my classmates, particularly the girls who tended to like boys who played sports rather than those who wrote good book reports. Of course, all this desire to play baseball was just fantasy of the highest order; my skills were only average at best, but my mind and imagination were working on overtime, so I hustled and kept on dreaming.

I was lucky and managed to survive yet another cut and on a blustery spring day trudged with thirty or thirty-five other hopefuls to a recently thawed mud-puddle-spattered field in a public park that was the home field of the Nottingham Bulldogs. It was now in the first week or ten days of April, and the competition was becoming serious. The number of uniforms determined the size of the team, and everyone knew there were just about twenty, maybe one or two more but probably less, and who knew how many had been ruined during the 1954 season?

The ball field in Thornton Park was what one might expect in a barely adequately maintained public park, but to my eyes, used to staring at the garage wall, wooden gymnasium floors, and a gravely parking lot, it looked like Yankee Stadium. There was a pitcher's mound, and while right field ended in trees and bushes about two hundred feet from home plate, center and left went on forever. There were only a few lefties among the better hitters, so I thought I might be able to keep them from hitting too many into the trees. And I was right. I got my hands on a horsehide-covered baseball with raised seams, threw real hard, mixed in my more than adequate knuckleball and dinky curve, and somehow managed to fool enough batters to make the next cut at the end of the week.

The number of kids left was decreasing, but I realized that almost none of those remaining were freshmen; most had been on the team the year before, and those who hadn't were known in school or were on some other team and known to the coaches. The other reality was that we were running out of time; scheduled games began in late April, and a complete team had to be assembled a week or two in advance of the "opening day" of the high school season.

I had another problem to contend with, one which made making the team doubly important: to be accepted at Nottingham High School, at least by the people I thought important, meant I had to be on one of three major teams, either football, basketball, or baseball. This was just my freshman year, but in my muddled mind I thought it might be my last chance for social acceptance. I knew I couldn't play the full baseball season even if I made the team; I had to leave school before the end of the semester to go with my father back to Indiana, where he was teaching at the university that summer. I also knew that at 6'2" and

140 pounds I was so skinny the only position I could make on the football team later in the year was possibly as a stand-in for one side of a goal post, and I didn't want to wait until basketball season. So this was my last chance for many months, if not forever. If I failed, not only would I face another year without organized baseball, but I'd be a social outcast as well, or so I imagined.

There were three groups of kids at my school: those who were on one of the three major teams, those who studied all the time, and the greasers. I wanted to be with the guys who played ball, especially the subculture within that group that not only could play a sport but also knew how to read and write. The nerds who studied all day weren't even clever enough to plot any kind of revenge, and the greasers who hung out on drugstore corners, dreaming of Elvis and the just-dead James Dean, were worse. One group wanted a circular slide rule and the other longed for fast bikes, slicked hair, and sloppy girls.

I could see the drugstore from my house and watched the greasers who hung out there, hoping a tight sweater might walk by. I watched the studious crowd suck up to everyone from the librarian to hall monitors. I didn't want to have anything to do with either, and the soon-to-be green outfield and dusty infield at Thornton Park was, I hoped, to be my salvation. As I look back on it maybe there were four groups at the school; the three I have mentioned plus another group of fools, of which I was a part—people who really felt it was important to be part of a certain group. Of course, it wasn't foolish to want to make the baseball team, but the social part was about as silly as the rebel without a clue crowd; I just didn't have enough sense to know it.

About the time all this foolishness was rattling around in my head where there were clearly far too many hormones bubbling about, stirring up all sorts of adolescent foolishness, Ty Cobb was busy attending to his daily chores of signing autographs for those who reached him by mail. One day that month the supposedly wicked old baseball player was moved again to be kind to an unknown correspondent, and he dispatched a large envelope toward Syracuse. As the envelope crossed the country by truck and train my struggle for a uniform was coming to an end, and the day of reckoning was at hand.

The uniforms were to be passed out after school on an anxious day in mid-April. There was no list of who made or didn't make the team. A far more cruel selection process had been devised. All those who hadn't been cut were instructed to report to a long hallway that led from the school's main corridor, past the offices occupied by various coaches, into the locker room. The uniforms were in the baseball coach's office, and after he felt everyone was present he called the name of one player he'd selected. The holdovers from the previous year were all called, one at a time. It was crucial to be called early because it meant a better uniform. Clearly, those chosen last would have to make do with whatever was left; a short kid might look silly in a uniform that hung to his ankles and a tall guy like myself would look stupid in pants that were too short, but not nearly as foolish as hanging out on a drugstore corner.

I was good in math and could count to twenty, a number that seemed to be coming up very quickly. More and more uniforms were passed out and still my name wasn't called. Finally Pat Stark, the baseball coach, stepped out of his office and announced number twenty, the final uniform, and it wasn't my name he called out, but that of another freshman. I was devastated and picked up my books to leave as the last player gleefully hurried into the office to pick up his uniform.

Then a funny thing happened: either I couldn't count or they had enough for twenty-one players, because the coach called my name. I tossed my books and ran down the hall to claim my prize, an ill-fitting, dingy gray uniform and a hat that was a size too small. I was certain this was the ultimate achievement of my short life. Now, over sixty years later, I still have the hat. It hangs from a nail in my cluttered darkroom. Now, however, a good deal of my hair has fallen out, and it fits somewhat better.

As it turned out I'd simply miscounted and wasn't nearly as smart as I thought; but no matter, the last uniform was mine. I looked ridiculous and I probably played only slightly better, but I'd managed to do what I set out to do. I'd made the team, and I was certain my future was not only secure, but would probably be remarkable, at least for the next four years. Nothing would make me give up that uniform. I've often wondered what became of it, and I honestly don't remember. I don't even remember the number on the back. Does Mickey Mantle's high school uniform still hang silently in the back of someone's closet in Commerce, Oklahoma? Possibly. Is it worth millions? Maybe.

So what if I'd been the last guy chosen; it made no difference. I could say goodbye to the garage wall, file away all my baseball magazines, and stash the bubblegum cards in a shoebox in the back of a closet. The autograph books were placed on a shelf out of reach. I could still see them from my desk, but the only real reminder of my days as a super fan was a color page torn from a magazine. It showed a smiling Bob Feller, tipping his cap, and was signed to me. It had hung on the wall since it came in the mail in 1953, and I decided to leave it there.

The other day I looked at those old autograph books and found the last one I started, the one that is only half full, dated summer 1955. The last autograph in the book, still not taped down, is George Sisler, a guy not much spoken of these days. Yet he hit over .400 twice and after fifteen seasons had a lifetime average of .340, which may well be higher than the best in either league in 2020. I don't know why Sisler's is the last one in the book; it had come in months earlier. I know because I saved the Pittsburgh Pirate envelope. I guess I just neglected to put it in the book.

But I was now busy with other things; I had reached the point where it was no longer necessary to keep autograph books or worry about what might turn up when I checked the milk box after school. After school was now for playing baseball, not writing letters about baseball to anyone. I was spending all the daylight hours after school making up for the two years of playing I'd lost. Sure, if an autograph came in the mail, and sometimes they took many months to arrive, I'd save it, and maybe I'd even go see the Chiefs play, but not very often, and I certainly didn't plan to hang out waiting for the players to come out of the clubhouse. There were just other things to do, mainly to hang out with the twenty other kids on the team.

I don't remember what was more thrilling. Was it coming home with the uniform and proudly showing my folks? Or was it getting out of class early to go play the first game of the season? Showing my special pass from the baseball coach to an unbelieving instructor or study hall monitor and waltzing out in front of all my peers. Hey! I made the team! I don't have to sit here in study hall and conjugate Latin verbs for the rest of the day. *Us A Um* to you and quick as a flash I'd vanish, running down the empty hallways toward the gymnasium.

I still remember the first game like it was yesterday. We suited up in the empty school locker room and then drove to the other side of town for the game. The coach took some players; his assistant took others. Older members of the team who had cars at school drove the rest, probably breaking a dozen school regulations and insurance policies in the process.

The enemy was a high school called simply "North," an imaginative name for a school on the north side of town, just a few blocks from the junior high where during the previous year I'd been incarcerated with hoards of juvenile, probably soon to become senior, delinquents. We played that first game on the Grant Junior High field, the same one where there was never a ballgame the year before except when an always justifiably wary, unwilling teacher faced an unruly, unwilling gym class, urging them to play softball. I told the guys the North team would be a pushover; I was surprised they could even find nine people to field as a team. Since I knew the territory, I suggested we'd better have someone guard the cars.

We beat them pretty good that day, and no one lost any hubcaps, but over the next three years this same team caused us a good deal of heartache. Still, we won that first one, and even though I didn't get to play, I couldn't have been happier. That I sat on the bench was a clear indication of things to come, but I didn't expect to play at all that first year unless at least half the team was injured. The truth is I didn't have to play to shock some of my former classmates at Grant Junior High; I just had to be there.

Many of these fledgling gangsters had failed eighth grade yet again, managing to avoid high school for another year. They could barely read or write, but how they could hang out, preferably where there was a crowd, smoking cigarettes—rough and ready guys who couldn't harmonize. It was heaven to be back on that junior high school field, in uniform, with a team that was thrashing their older brothers. Who knows, maybe that was my biggest baseball thrill, seeing the looks of disbelief on their faces. That day was over sixty years ago, and I still remember it like it happened an hour ago, but I'm probably the only one who does. In the early 1990s I went back to Syracuse and made certain I had time to have possibly one last look at one of my fields of dreams. It looked pretty good, and I took a picture. In 2020 Google Earth reveals a rather tattered field that needs some tender love and care and has probably not been game used for some years.

Then another letter turned up, the one Ty Cobb sent about the time I was collecting my uniform. I don't remember exactly when it arrived but it was probably in late April, at least that's when it's dated, around the time of that first game on the north side of town. It was in a large brown envelope with my name in green ink on the mailing label. Ty Cobb had written to me again and the envelope turned out to be full of treasures. He'd not only signed the page I'd clipped from a small booklet I'd bought at the Hall of Fame, but he'd sent me a large 8"x10" photograph as well, written a serious two-page letter, and then added a long three-page postscript not only explaining the photograph but asking me a favor and suggesting that I write him about the event captured in the photograph. Then everything changed.

Here was Ty Cobb, a man vilified by writers and players alike, a man whose reputation as a baseball player was second to none but who was regarded by almost everyone as only slightly better than Hitler in the humanity department. In his letter, and in giving me the photograph, he is being kind, inquisitive, helpful, and fascinating. He reveals much about himself. He couldn't be a better person, giving of his time, his thoughts, his possessions, asking little in return. And what do I do? Absolutely nothing!

Cobb asked only that I order a certain issue of the *Sporting News* and even told me how to get the copy for free. He still knew how to work the system! Do I get the paper? NO! Do I even write him back? I don't think so. Maybe I did, but I don't think so, and if I did, I clearly didn't address the question he asked me at the end of the note. Now, who's the bum? Certainly not Ty Cobb. He's done all he could, writing me letters that in their own way were very encouraging; he sent me a photograph that still hangs on my office wall. He provided the raw material for this memoir.

But in April 1955 I was a little too swollen with pride and excitement, too busy sitting on the bench, the last man on the Nottingham Bulldog's baseball team. I just didn't have the time to answer a letter from Ty Cobb. My guess is that my bad manners didn't bother him much in 1955, but in 2020 it still bothers the hell out of me. Why, I ask myself, was I such a jerk? Maybe for the same reason big-time baseball players today are often too busy for some kid looking for an autograph. It's easy to be a jerk, whether you're playing in Yankee Stadium or in a muddy public park.

I didn't think I was so terrible in 1955. I probably didn't think about what I did (or didn't do) at all, but the truth is I just didn't write to any baseball players after I made the team; when I was playing, even as last man, playing was all that was on my mind. And besides, I was afraid my teammates would think I was weird and even younger than fourteen if they knew I was such a fan. None of them chased baseball players; at least I'd never seen any of them in the MacArthur Stadium bleachers or hanging out in back of the clubhouse. Maybe they all chased them on different days and also kept it a secret, but my guess is that I was the only one of twenty who'd hung out in the lobby of the Onondaga Hotel looking for players or attended meetings of the local Hot Stove League to listen to the then seventy-five-year-old George "Hooks" Wiltse talk about his ten-inning Fourth of July no-hitter against Philadelphia in 1908 and his years with John McGraw's glorious New York Giants around the turn of the century. But once I made the team, my days as a super fan were officially over.

LOST SEASONS

I didn't officially finish the 1955 spring semester at Nottingham and probably missed a couple of games, but my father had a summer school assignment at the University of Indiana and we had to leave in early June for him to begin his teaching schedule. Since he was the assistant superintendent of schools, there was no difficulty in obtaining a "get out of school early" pass. I thought this was terrific.

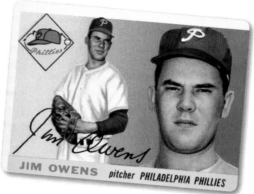

Now that I was out of town, it was possible to be a fan again; I couldn't be caught and embarrassed by any of my older teammates if I was hundreds of miles away. But this was the last year I bought bubblegum cards and, as I recall, there was no difficulty in finding all the cards for a complete set. For some reason Topps only had 210 cards that year, a big reduction from over 400 in 1952, and considerably fewer than the 280 in 1953 and 250 in 1954. I had managed to find all the cards from 1953 and 1954, so it was easy to come up with 210 before I returned home in the fall. One of the last cards in the series featured Jim Owens, whom I'd seen in Syracuse the previous two years. I didn't know it then, but I'd see him a couple of months later in a Philadelphia uniform.

This was also the summer I managed to accumulate all the old cigarette cards from Wirt Gammon. I had more dimes than usual and I spent most of them with him, in the years when George Browne cost the same as Mordecai Brown, even though one was a famous Hall of Fame pitcher and the other didn't even have his name spelled correctly on his card.

Hoosier Courts would be our home once again, but because my father was now teaching a course we were housed in newly built garden apartments. But down at the bottom on the hill, the big green field was still there, and there were lots of kids and the games went on and on, but somehow it was different. The broken-down backstop was missing and so was the university team, so there were no loose baseballs in the weeds or broken bats. Even though I was a much better player now, the games, which only occurred infrequently, weren't as special as they'd been a couple of years earlier. What was special, however, was a daytrip to Cincinnati on August 4. My parents went shopping, and I went to Crosley Field.

Had to send these cards.
Have no list. Suggest putting up
a deposit for approval lots.
Please include postage on orders
under $2.

WIRT GAMMON
812 MOUNT VERNON CIRCLE
CHATTANOOGA 5, TENN.

PHILADELPHIA VS. CINCINNATI—AUGUST 4, 1955

August 4, 1955, an ordinary Thursday afternoon, in an ordinary city in southern Ohio. It was sunny and bright, an ideal day for a baseball game between a couple of teams who weren't in contention, but who could play a great game on any given day. There were stars galore on each team, and I was excited.

In the early 1950s, Cincinnati was my favorite National League team. This was due to geography. Cincinnati was only a couple of hundred miles from Bloomington, Indiana, and the hometown television station regularly broadcast Cincinnati games. Waite Hoyt, a future Hall of Famer, did the broadcasting chores, plugging the local sponsor, Burger Beer. *This is the Burger Beer Broadcasting Network*, he intoned with authority. And then they'd play Sousa's "El Capitan March" with new lyrics urging the listener to *Buy Burger, Buy Burger*.

But those broadcasts were a couple of years earlier, and now I knew more about the Philadelphia Phillies and some of their players. I was now an official resident of Syracuse, and the Syracuse Chiefs were Philadelphia's Triple-A farm club. A few of the players with the Phillies in 1955 had been with Syracuse in 1953 and 1954, guys like Bob Micelotta and Jack Meyer, so I had mixed loyalties. My guess is I cheered for each team equally.

I don't have any recollection of who won that day, or if there were any outstanding moments, but sixty-five years later, thanks to the internet, I can type in the date with the words "Philadelphia vs. Cincinnati," and the box score pops up, crammed with details and facts. Cincinnati won, 4-3; Wally Post and Del Ennis hit home runs; and Jack Meyer, whom I'd seen in Syracuse, pitched in relief. I also learned I was one of 2,793 fans in the stands that day, which wasn't much of a crowd. So much for the facts, thanks to the internet, but facts are mainly important to historians; memories are much more real and the first thing I remember is this was just the second major league game I'd ever seen in person, and this time I was better prepared than I was when I saw Cleveland play St. Louis a couple of years earlier.

By prepared, I mean I was armed with dozens of slips of paper and a couple of ballpoint pens, hoping to get an autograph or two after

the game. I had no idea it would turn out the way it did, and what happened was remarkable, at least to me. The same thing may have happened to hundreds of kids every day, all summer long, after hundreds of ball games, which is why they waited patiently outside the clubhouse door, waiting for their heroes to emerge. But this was my first and only time, and I could never have anticipated what happened. It is a wonderful memory and to me far more important than the game and who won or lost. My guess is the experience I had doesn't happen very often in 2020, if at all, but I certainly enjoyed it on that August afternoon, probably as much as I enjoyed the game.

My parents had left me alone at Crosley Field, promising to come back and pick me up in the parking lot at a given time. I don't remember if the game went very quickly or if they were late, but I found myself waiting in the parking lot for what was probably an eternity, but which seemed like a few minutes. The time sped by. In fact, there wasn't enough time to do everything that needed to be done.

The ballplayers, coaches, and managers made their way out of their respective clubhouses into the parking lot. Bright-eyed kids, with their autograph books open and pens held high, descended upon most of them. I was one of those kids. Thank goodness the players didn't all come out at the same time; I wouldn't have had a chance. But they straggled out, one or two at a time, and by the time everyone was gone and the parking lot was almost empty, I'd managed to collect twenty-seven signatures. This is who signed my slips of paper:

Philadelphia	Cincinnati
Wally Moses	Joe Nuxall
Whitlow Wyatt	Jerry Staley
Del Ennis	Ted Kluszewski
Herman Wehmeier	Wally Post
Ed Waitkus	Roy McMillan
Willie Jones	Gus Bell
Andy Seminick	Johnny Temple
Granny Hamner	Birdie Tebbets
Roy Smalley	Dick Bartell
Robin Roberts	Johnny Klippstein
Ron Negray	
Stan Lopata	
Bob Micelotta	
Richie Ashburn	
Marv Blalock	
Jimmy Greenglass	
Benny Bengough	

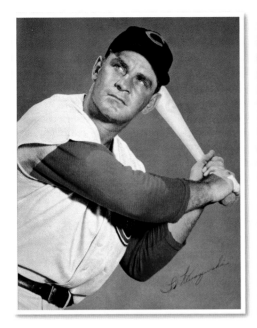

The twenty-seven slips of paper later made their way to a waiting autograph book and joined the bubblegum cards and pictures from magazines that came from correspondence and had turned up in my mailbox.

My main memory of that afternoon in the parking lot is that when all the players had left, there was one man who remained, leaning against his car, with a hoard of eager kids surrounding him. It was Ted Kluszewski. He was wearing a short-sleeve shirt, a flowery version of the cut-off uniform he often wore on the field. His arms seemed larger than the bodies of the kids surrounding him. I watched him sign everything that was offered up. It was finally my turn, and he signed a piece of paper. My parents finally arrived, and as we drove away I looked back and he was still standing there, surrounded by eager kids.

Kluszewski's pretty much forgotten now, but that year he led the league in hits and was second only to Willie Mays in home runs and total bases. The year before he led the league in home runs, runs batted in, and home run percentage. He was a big deal in those days, yet there he was standing in the parking lot, after a long game and signing something for everyone who asked, until there was no one left. I didn't see it happen, but when the last kid was gone, he probably just got in his car and drove off. No posse, no security, no limo, just a car like every other one in the parking lot. Maybe a little better than average, but not much, and certainly no chemical-induced histrionics, on field or off.

Kluszewski hit forty-nine home runs in 1954 and forty-seven in 1955, and he did it without any artificial help. The steroid-pumped guys of the 1990s and 2000s and the hundred dollar or more autograph guys of today could learn something from him.

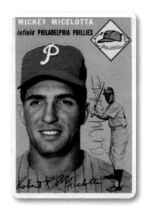

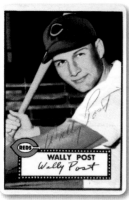

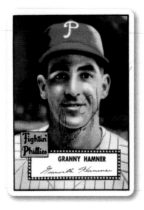

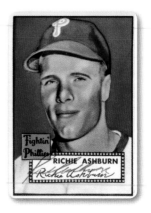

⤳ BACK HOME, 1956 ⤳

Events become a little fuzzy after that first game and the first season, and my high school years are muddled and race by in my mind. But some events pop up now and again, leading up to my final year of baseball. After that first game with North about all I recall is we were not very good, maybe a game or two over .500. We won more than we lost but not

Nottingham's MacLachlan Hurls 3rd No-Hitter

Bulldogs Top Central, 5-0 Regain Lead

Eastwood Held To One Hit by North's Rossi

many more. The next year, 1955-56 we were better, a lot better.

In the spring of 1956, we were invincible. It was our glory year, and presumably the trophy we won still sits in a case in the now middle-aged-getting-older school building at the end of Meadowbrook Drive. We were an exceptionally good team, so good, particularly in the pitching department, that I rarely saw any activity at all. We had a couple of pitchers who were very good and another who was truly remarkable. The remarkable one was a tall, gangly kid named Bill MacLachlan. He seemed to pitch a no-hitter or a shutout every time he took the mound. When he pitched, we won; it was as simple as that. When someone else pitched we usually won, but it was harder.

The local papers ran enormous headlines and stories about his prowess, and on the final day of the season he pitched a one-hit shutout to secure the league championship. A week or so later he pitched another one-hit shutout to beat Cathedral, the parochial league champions, and we won the city championship. The headline in the *Syracuse Post-Standard* of June 12, 1956, read: "Nottingham Defeats Cathedral 3-0 for City Title." Needless to say, I didn't get to play that day.

There were some very fine players on the 1956 team; some were scouted by major league teams, some minor bonuses were offered, but no one ever got any higher than Triple-A, and I don't know what happened to any of them. They probably took off their uniforms, graduated, maybe went to college; perhaps they didn't, but most probably lived ordinary lives which, hopefully, they still enjoy. Except for one person, on a single occasion, I've never been in touch with any of them.

On a personal level this high standard of schoolyard play meant I pitched a lot of batting practice, shagged flies, took my turn at bat, never missed a practice or a game, envied the guys who could have a date with Judy on springtime days after school, and once almost died when I saw a girl I hoped to win over making out in the bushes with an arch rival while I was chasing down a baseball. He was already to second base and heading towards third and I was still very much in the outfield. How I wished they'd found a wider tree to hide behind for their afternoon tryst.

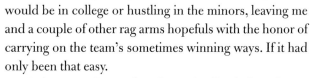

14 THE POST-STANDARD, Syracuse, N. Y., Tuesday, June 12, 1956

Nottingham Defeats Cathedral, 3-0, for City Title

MacLachlan Hurls 1 Hitter, Helps at Bat

Bangs Two Hits Off Burke, One A Triple for Run

Then it was the spring of 1957, and we spent some time practicing at the same often-muddy field. I was a year older, had gained a little weight, and was throwing harder and with more accuracy, but by and large I pitched batting practice that year most of the time, and I rarely got into a game unless we were way ahead, which wasn't that often. Bill MacLachlan, the guy with the big fastball and swooping curve, had graduated, but there were lots of guys in front of me. If things were really lopsided I might get to pitch an inning or two, but I pinch-hit or was a pinch runner far more often than I ever pitched. To make matters worse, we didn't win the league championship that year; we lost it on the final day of the season and came in second place.

All I could think was at least I didn't lose that final game, and I was part of a fine team. There was always 1958, and I looked forward to my final year, when all the hotshot pitchers would be in college or hustling in the minors, leaving me and a couple of other rag arms hopefuls with the honor of carrying on the team's sometimes winning ways. If it had only been that easy.

In between, I got to be a fan again, if only for a day. In July I visited Cooperstown for the second time to attend a Hall of Fame induction ceremony and the annual Hall of Fame Game.

THE HALL OF
FAME GAME

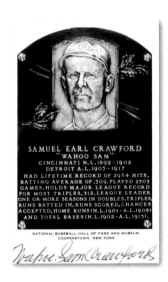

SAMUEL EARL CRAWFORD
"WAHOO SAM"
CINCINNATI N.L. 1899-1902
DETROIT A.L. 1903-1917
HAD LIFETIME RECORD OF 2964 HITS,
BATTING AVERAGE OF .309. PLAYED 2505
GAMES. HOLDS MAJOR LEAGUE RECORD
FOR MOST TRIPLES, 312. LEAGUE LEADER
ONE OR MORE SEASONS IN DOUBLES, TRIPLES,
RUNS BATTED IN, RUNS SCORED, CHANCES
ACCEPTED, HOME RUNS (N.L. 1901 - A.L. 1908)
AND TOTAL BASES (N.L. 1902 - A.L. 1913).
NATIONAL BASEBALL HALL OF FAME AND MUSEUM
COOPERSTOWN, NEW YORK

My second trip to the National Baseball Hall of Fame was on July 21, 1957. The idea was to visit other museums in Cooperstown on Friday and then see the Hall of Fame inductions, as well as the Sixteenth Annual Hall of Fame Game at Doubleday Field, on Saturday.

The inductees that year were Sam Crawford and Joe McCarthy. I stood in the crowd and managed to take one picture with my Brownie Hawkeye. If you look carefully, you can see Sam Crawford on the steps. About all I remember of the ceremony is that it wasn't very crowded. You can see that from my snapshot.

Later, my father and I went to the game and sat in the outfield bleachers, watching the Chicago White Sox skunk the St. Louis Cardinals 13-4. I took another snapshot, but I was too far away from the action to tell what was going on. My big disappointment was that Stan Musial didn't play that day. I had written his number on my scorecard, but he didn't play. For some reason he had the day off, perhaps knowing full well he'd be back in a few years to be inducted. Too bad for me; it was the only chance I had to see him live and it was the last year he won the batting championship.

☙ THE LAST SEASON ❧

In the spring of 1958, I was served up a reality sandwich. I was slated to be a starter in my senior year, if for no other reason than because there were so few pitchers on the team, but it was not to be; fate was unkind. Perhaps I was punished for not responding to Ty Cobb's last letter.

The twenty uniforms were passed out in mid-April and serious practice began, but at the beginning of the season, when a few nonleague games were scheduled, all those selected as pitchers had either minor injuries or were down with the flu except for one: me. I was healthy and throwing well, so I found myself busy on the mound. The fastball was zipping along; my nickel curve was up to a dime; my usually uncontrollable screwball sometimes even confused my coach; and I still fooled with a knuckleball just for fun. I was overjoyed; this was going to be my year, and Coach Stark even occasionally passed a compliment my way. But trouble, great big sore-arm trouble, was just a few days away, and I was suddenly too busy on the mound.

I got the nod to pitch the first of our unofficial games. I did well enough this first time out, took off a day, and was on the mound again with but one day's rest for our next game. I endured the seven innings, but I ached a little more than usual after the game. The next day one of our other pitchers was less flu-ridden and started, thank goodness, but he just lasted a few innings and faded. Warm up, I was told, and I did as I was told.

It was a windy, cold, overcast April day. The Thornton Park field was muddy and dangerous, with standing puddles of water here and there. Why, I wondered, were we even playing? This was just a practice game. I warmed up as best I could but didn't last an inning. I tried to throw as hard as possible, but it wasn't very hard at all, and I was pounded. Nothing worked. I was confused and feeling useless.

Maybe I should try throwing junky curves, I thought, but then something went pop in my elbow the first time I tried one. I'd never felt pain like that in my arm; I knew instantly I'd done something awful. The catcher threw the ball back to me; surprisingly I caught it but I couldn't hold the ball in my right hand. I couldn't even straighten out my arm to take the ball out of my glove. I was absolutely terrified. Time was called, play was halted, and I wandered off the mound in pain and a daze. Little was said; I just sat there in the cold. My sports medicine prescription was not to pitch anymore that afternoon.

This was the first time my arm had ever been hurt and it really bothered me, but it never occurred to me that I wouldn't get better and get better fast. The intense pain finally went away after a few days and I was able to straighten my arm, and soon I was even able to throw a little. Slowly, I tried to get back in shape, but the season, which wasn't very long, was racing by. We were still winning, but not on the strength of our pitching. Thank goodness we still had guys who could pile on the runs.

I still don't know what I did to my arm, except to use it too much too early in the season, but it soon became clear the damage was far more serious than I suspected. It took a lot of the joy out of the game for me. It was no longer just fun and excitement. It was trying to endure. I couldn't throw a curve without intense shooting pains running up from my elbow into my upper arm. I had lost some speed, mainly the hop on the fastball, but I could still throw moderately hard and my knuckleball danced on windy days.

On the outside I acted like I could still help the team, but I was smart enough to know that a lame fastball and a windblown knuckler was a pretty sorry combination of pitches. Coach Stark also knew. He might not have known about letting me pitch so much early in the year, but he could easily recognize someone who was basically trying to fake it. He could see I wasn't that fast and the knuckler didn't jump around like Hoyt Wilhelm's. And forget my screwball. It didn't hurt when I twisted my arm in the opposite direction from a curve ball motion, but after I was hurt, my screwball was about as reliable as my teenage hormones.

So it was relief duty for the rest of the year, an inning or two, every other game. I almost got to start one game because the wind was blowing the right way for a knuckleball, but when the wind died, so did my chances. That was the bad news; the good was that we were a decent team that year and we had a chance to win the championship once again. We also had a chance at something special; at least it was special to me.

The Syracuse Chiefs left town in 1955 and MacArthur Stadium was vacant. The local Board of Education had petitioned the mayor to allow some high school games to be played at the now-abandoned ballpark. After the usual bureaucratic bickering, arrangements were made for all the local teams to use the stadium at least once a season, and the Nottingham team looked forward to the day we'd get to play on the best ball field in town.

We got off to a good start, winning most of our games, and by mid-May we were leading the league with a six and one record. I was doing little more than making an occasional relief appearance for an inning or two, or sometimes I was stuck in as a pinch runner or hitter. Limited duty on the field; long-time duty on the bench, and then it came our time to play at the stadium.

Leaders Keep Going In City Baseball

The league leaders all won in the City Baseball League yesterday. Nottingham walloped three Smith Tech pitchers to retain their top spot, winning by a 14-0 margin.

Other scores were: Central 2, Eastwood 1; North 1, Valley 0; CBA 2, Vocational 1.

Nottingham, which won its ninth in 11 games, got some heavy sticking from Mike Humphrey, Dick DeLeon and Howie Garelick to coast to the easy victory.

Smith Tech.... 0 0 0 0 0 0 0—0 3 3
Nottingham.... 1 1 2 2 x—14 9 1
Nasy, Fritzen (2), Sullivan, and P: raino, Miller DeLeon (5), O'Nell (7) and Burns, Pardee (6).

Official Stadium Opening Tonight

City and high school officials will try again tonight to officially open the gates of MacArthur Stadium for scholastic baseball.

Although City and Parochial League nines have already performed this season at the park, the official opening of the stadium was rescheduled for tonight at 8 p.m. Ceremonies were originally planned for last Saturday but the program was cancelled by rain.

A City League game between Eastwood and Central will open tonight's program at 6:30 p.m. Parochial League rivals Cathedral and St. John the Baptist clash at 8:30.

Participants in tonight's formal ceremonies include Mayor Anthony Henninger, who will pitch the first ball to John Kane, member of the Board of Education; Dr. Paul Miller, superintendent of Syracuse public schools; the Rt. Rev. Msgr. James Callaghan, superintendent of Parochial schools; Lew Andreas, Syracuse University athletic director; Charles Stover, head of the city's physical education department; the Rev. Frank Sammons of the CYO office and Francis Judkins, recently named superintendent of MacArthur Stadium activities.

Nottingham Nine Takes School Lead

I was going to possibly play at MacArthur Stadium; maybe I wouldn't get in the game, but it would be a thrill just to walk onto the field, to sit in the dugout, or even pitch batting practice. I was going to revisit my past, my childhood, which seemed as long ago as forever, even though it was only four years. This was, after all, the same place I'd chased all those young International League stars a few years earlier, pleading for an autograph.

I hadn't been inside the old ballpark in almost three years. When the Chiefs left town there was no reason to go, but as our team walked through the opening in the right field wall onto the field, I was a little shaken because I'd never set foot on the playing field. When I'd first stood behind the chain-link fence, that fence, asking any player who might walk by for an autograph, I never really thought I'd ever make it to the other side and walk onto the field to play a game. I hesitated for a moment as memories came flooding back. I'd just turned eighteen and was anything but sloppy and sentimental, but couldn't help but be struck by the irony of it all.

I knew that stepping onto the MacArthur Stadium outfield was some sort of culmination of events for me, the end of one part of my life and perhaps the beginning of something else. This was where I'd arrived, standing in the outfield of MacArthur Stadium after a few years of childhood and teenage play. I thought of the parched Texas fields and the lot down by the tracks in Indiana, all those games of pickle in the front yard, hurling a battered baseball at the garage wall and chasing and catching a piece of youthful college heroes, International League stars, and certified Hall of Fame immortals. Of course, I also thought about four years of mediocre high school ball and ending up with a lame arm. All sorts of thoughts and emotions jumped around in my head as I walked slowly toward the dugout. I knew full well that unless we made our way to play for the city championship, this was the only time I'd make this walk.

No one stuck a piece of paper through the fence for me or anyone else to sign. We had no spectators; there were no eager fans in the stands to cheer us on. No overzealous parent to hurl obscenities at the umpire or opposing players or to cheer on their offspring. MacArthur Stadium was miles from our high school and probably just as far away from our opponent's headquarters. This was no surprise; no one came to the games that were close to home, except for a player's girlfriend every so often and the stragglers who might be in the park that day. So why would anyone come across town on a wonderful sunny spring day with the school year coming to a close?

There were more important things to do, and most kids, including almost everyone on the baseball team, were far more interested in sneaking a drink of tequila at the

Nottingham, Central Clash at Stadium

Second half play in the City High School Baseball League opens tonight at MacArthur Stadium with Nottingham's pacesetters taking on last place Central. Game time is 6:30 p.m.

hop, watching girls in short shorts, or cruising around town with the top down being a rabble rouser with the sound of Duane Eddy's guitar blasting from the car's puny three-inch speakers. We wanted to win the game as quickly as possible and a couple of others and be done with the season so we could spend as much time as we could with all the good friends we'd made during the past four years, people we knew we'd probably rarely see again after graduation, unless we were confined to Syracuse for the rest of our lives, and few of us thought we would.

Our opponent was a school named Central, then the largest school in the city, but not one known for athletics. The game wasn't a romp, but we won four to two, and just a few details stand out, like when the tide turned as first fullback-outfielder Mike Humphrey stole home and then our beefy first baseman, Pete Palumb, did the same thing, trampling the opposing catcher in a cloud of dust. This was not a nice thing to do, but he was also a football hero when not on first base, and used to such antics. This seemed to demoralize our opponents, and Coach Stark was so confident we'd win he told me to go warm up to pitch the final inning. This was a nice gesture.

I went down to the bullpen with a teammate, took off my jacket, and began to work the kinks out of my virtually useless right arm. I was as ready as I could be by the time we took the field for what we assumed would be the last inning.

I walked in from the right field bullpen past the empty bleachers and an equally empty grandstand and made my way to the pitcher's mound. I stood there for a moment and just looked around the large but now somewhat moth-eaten ballpark. I hoped the guys in the field were ready to run, because whatever stuff I once had was just a memory. They knew it too.

It turned out they didn't have to work too hard, and my last hurrah was an uneventful inning. Baseball can be like that; bad hitters can pound good pitchers and some days luck is with a rag arm facing decent players. You just never know. They got a base runner or two but things worked out, and while no one threatened to score there was at least one runner left on base when I faced the last batter.

I dished up some junk in his direction, he swung and lifted a high infield fly off to the right of the pitcher's mound. I should have moved out of the way and let the third baseman grab the ball, but I wanted the last out so I hollered "it's mine!" I watched the ball go up, peak and start down. I heard the third baseman yell at me, as he should have, but I made the play anyway. The game was over and I walked off the field, clutching the baseball, one that I should have kept but didn't. I picked up my warmup jacket and walked through the door in the right field wall, knowing I'd never pass that way again.

We were still leading the league, but a couple of other teams were nipping at our heels. Then we lost a couple and suddenly we found ourselves in second place, a game back. We were scheduled to play the Valley Academy on my birthday, June 5. Their team was mediocre at best, an easy opponent, and it seemed likely I'd get an extra present that day.

We pounded them and when the outcome was certain, I was called in to pitch an inning or so, to conserve more reliable arms for the final game of the season, which would be the next day. I remember the skies were dark and it was windy. Rain was on its way. We were way ahead, and if the rains came the game would count, whether I pitched or not. I took a leisurely walk to the mound, fiddled with the rubber, and decided that it wasn't going to pour for a while so I'd better make the best of the wind and lack of light. I knew the only pitches I had were my now hopeless hard one and an increasingly unreliable knuckler, which today might be even more unpredictable in the now almost gale-force wind swirling around the field.

After a few warm-up tosses I glanced at the first batter, the opposing pitcher. He should be easy, I thought, and he swung through the first two barely adequate pitches I threw in his direction. Thank goodness he didn't hit any better than he pitched. Brimming with confidence I decided to serve up my very best knuckler and it turned out to be a dandy one, jumping around in the dimming late afternoon light through clouds of swirling dust stirred up from the wind-blown infield. The only problem was the pitch was about two feet inside and heading straight for the no doubt terrified pitcher holding on to his bat with trembling hands. He tried to get out of the way as best as possible, but the pitch was dead on-target and there was no way he could dodge it.

All this looked funny from my perspective; the hapless batter looked like a cartoon character dodging a ball and no matter where he went it chased him down, finally smacking him in the middle of the back. No harm was done, he wasn't hurt at all—who would have been by a barely thirty mile per hour knuckler dancing in the wind?—but I realized this was the wrong guy to nail, even with a dinky pitch. I was scheduled to lead off the next inning and now Valley's pitcher was doubly sore. My teammates had been pounding him all day and now I've hit him in the back. I was certain he would try to put one in my ear.

I got through the inning with no other problems, but as I walked off the field and began thinking about leading off the inning, Coach Stark had the good sense to send in a pinch hitter for me and not give the guy I'd just hit the opportunity to whack me. He let our catcher, Don Burns, who was also a pretty good pitcher, work the final inning. I was relieved to be relieved and was sitting on the bench when the long-delayed rains finally came.

The next day we were back at Thornton Park to play our archrivals, the hated Christian Brothers Academy. If we won, we'd be tied for first place and a playoff would be in order. If we lost, the season was over. We lost, shut out for the first time all year. The mainstay of our pitching staff, Fred Miller, pitched shutout ball for the regulation game, but he tired in the eighth inning and got pounded. There was no one left for relief duties other than me, so I went in once more, but this time under different circumstances. If we were to have any chance I had to retire the side before they piled on too many runs. I did, but it made no difference; we didn't even get a base runner in the final inning and the season was over. I sat

Nottingham Can Gain Tie With North

CBA Blocks Path Of East Siders

on the bench for a while, getting up the energy to walk home. There was no need to hitch a ride since it was no more than a fifteen-minute walk, and besides, I didn't feel like hanging out with anyone.

I stood around until everyone was gone and took a long last look. I'd made the team four years earlier by playing adequately on this field, and the team had some success there over the years. A couple of months earlier I'd ruined my arm on that miserable day in late April, and now we'd lost the championship, shut out on our home field. I'd pitched the last inning of the season, but we'd lost; it wasn't a good day or a place to remember.

I sat down on the bench and slowly changed my shoes and headed home. I was in no hurry, but I still took the short cut through the woods and underbrush in right field. The girl wasn't waiting for me behind a tree, but neither was my rival. I never played another game, but I'd had a pretty good run. I'd made the jump from a child playing in a field of weeds with planks and stones as bases in Texas to an almost grown-up, catching the final out in a game at Triple-A MacArthur Stadium, where just a few years before I'd marveled at soon-to-be heroes of tomorrow playing on their way up, and older faded heroes on their way down. All of this in less than a decade. Not bad, even if I didn't go out on a high note, owning an arm so limp it would flap with the slightest breeze.

And yet, even though it is now over sixty years later, on most days, if I have a moment for quiet reflection, and cast a glance at that picture of Ty Cobb on my office wall, I remember those days with great and growing affection. When Dylan Thomas suggested *the memories of childhood have no order*, he should have added that the memories of young adulthood are not much more orderly and perhaps even stronger.

TY COBB'S REQUEST,
⌘ APRIL 1955 ⌘

TYRUS R. COBB

Harold:— The picture I
send is of the so.
called Baker spiking
which I was so
unfairly accused of
by a drunken sports
writer Horace Fogel
on some Phila. paper
this play was in Detroit
so he writes a lurid
story really to arouse
the fans in Phila so
when Detroit came there
next, would boost
the attendance — this
has been a practice by
the unscrocupulous
writers, I have always

A STORY THAT RANKLED 46 YEARS
⤳ TY COBB ⤳
Rips Into Accusation of Infamous Spiking

By Ty Cobb
As Told to Jack McDonald, Sports
Editor of San Francisco Call-Bulletin
Menlo Park, Calif.

I have been asked by several sources to comment on the wisdom of selecting different players for the great honor of having been voted in baseball's Hall of Fame at Cooperstown, N. Y. I have always tried to give honest personal opinions.

Now I am asked to comment on the choice of Frank Baker, third baseman of the Philadelphia Athletics for so many years. My answer is that no selection could have been better and that Frank richly deserves this great honor that has come to him, in recognition of his years of sterling play.

I am truly happy for him that he was so selected. This man acquired the popular nickname of "Home Run." As one of the old-timers with the dead ball he succeeded in leading the American League by hitting 12 home runs in 1913. In fact, he led the league four straight years, in 1911 with nine, in 1912 with 10, in 1913 with 12 and in 1914 with eight.

So much for the old ball we old-timers used to hit. It's easy to see why the Baker of that day, with all his other qualifications, earned the right to his recent selection to the Hall of Fame.

In connection with Baker there was an episode back in August 1909, a game played in Detroit—the so-called infamous spiking of Baker by Cobb.

A very lurid story was written about it at the time by one Horace Fogel, a Philadelphia sports writer. As to Fogel's account of the event, I say unqualifiedly that in this story he was not out of character. He seemed to seek to arouse the venom of the fans, possibly working in the interest of the Philadelphia Athletic ball club, on the theory it might help their box office in Philadelphia, which did not enjoy rich patronage. It is not for me to make this charge.

On our next trip to Philadelphia I will say Fogel succeeded, beyond all expectations. Possibly Fogel and those of the Philadelphia club did not know or realize that I received 13 threatening letters. Some threatened assault with deadly weapons if I attempted to play in the series.

Well, it so happened that I did play all the games of this series. The fans were rabid. The crowd on the field was not far from my position in right field. I did happen to jump the boundary ropes and into the crowd, and by luck succeeded in catching about four balls.

Still Resents Charge of Intentional Spiking

I am now 68 years old. I still resent the charge of brutal and intentional spiking. This incident, remember, happened in 1909. This is 1955, and to this day, in meeting some young boy interested in baseball and whose father I might have met, I have been told: "Oh, you're the man who spiked Baker."

Now I am very fond of kids and try to do my share in Little League work, also at Boy Scout meetings, and really it presents me with an unpleasant situation.

Remembering if I had been guilty I would take it as coming to me. But let's examine the photograph of the play, which you see on this page. Note that Baker is clearly on the baseline and ON THE OFFENSIVE, with arms extended to tag me. I am pulling away but trying to reach the bag. Particularly note that my foot has passed by his right forearm, and the force of the so-called spiking has not even moved his arm from its position.

From the story, one would think I had knocked Baker's arm clear around behind his back and that he was lying on the ground from its force, and bleeding terribly. When, by records, which can be looked up, Frank Baker did not lose an inning of play, and continued, I am quite certain, in every game for the rest of the season.

To tell the truth, I did not even know Baker was injured in the slight way that he was. No one gathered around him, and he continued in the game.

Without any malice whatever towards Baker, because he might not have thought of doing what I feel he should have under the circumstances of the Fogel story, I must secretly confess I was disappointed that he didn't make a proper statement exonerating me of any intentional spiking. It would have placated the wild reception I received on the occasion of Detroit's next trip to Philadelphia.

So now, as above, I salute Frank Baker as a member of the Hall of Fame, and again say I am very happy that he has been so elected.

I can truthfully say that I have tried to spike only two men in all my years in baseball.

I have been thrown at many times. The only defense against this is to drag a bunt towards first base, so as to have the first baseman handle the ball, forcing the pitcher to cover first base and then to pile into him.

The practice of crying about it, and crying to the umpire, or your manager, or to the newspapers, was not my way. They can't handle the situation. The batter, who might have his skull cracked, or be killed, has to retaliate and put the fear of God in the offending pitcher's heart. At least, I found this was the most effective method.

To be decently delicate I refuse to mention the two pitchers. But the procedure I used in both instances was very effective and a complete cure of the situation was affected. In one of the instances I crowded the plate and I was pitched outside to afterward and drew many a walk, until this man came to me and apologized and wanted to call it off, which I was happy to do.

Honest Man Never Fears Consequences

In all my years in baseball, now, in the evening of my life, I would like to make one comment. In baseball, or any other game, or profession, or way of life, it is my deep conviction that when a man is honest and with honor, and aligns himself over what he thinks is the side of right, he can be the boldest and bravest, and never fear the consequences. This was my creed throughout my 24 years of major league play.

Never in my baseball experience have I been accused by a player on or off the field, or any issue made over any spiking. Also, strange to say of those days of years ago, there were few if any fisticuffs by individuals or team gathering, with an exchange of blows in the presence of spectators.

And finishing, let me say that to steal a base, the conclusive fact is that the base runner is trying to reach the bag by eluding the baseman's tag, and to do this successfully he must give only his toe or foot to tag.

It is been said that I developed the so-called fall away and fade-away slide. I have made no such claims myself, but if true in this way of sliding, one foot has to be on the ground, with the bag tagged with the toe, which places the spikes away from contact with the baseman.

Ty Cobb

AUTHOR'S NOTE:

In 2005 my friend Nick Niles was the president of the *Sporting News*. We were talking baseball one day, and I mentioned Ty Cobb's request fifty years earlier in 1955. He managed to find the old issue in the company archives and gave me a copy of Cobb's article and permission to use it in *Sincerely, Ty Cobb*. I read it with interest and then I wrote a letter, answering his questions as best I could, fifty years late. When I wrote the letter, I thought it would be amusing to use an old typewriter typeface, one that would duplicate the type on the typewriter my father had in 1955.

HANK O'NEAL

April 25, 2oo5

Mr. Ty Cobb
48 Spencer Lane, Atherton
Menlo Park, California

Dear Mr. Cobb,

Thanks so much for your wonderful letter and the terrific picture. I'm sorry it has taken me so long to reply, but the very day your letter arrived I made my high school baseball team, the youngest and least experienced player on the squad. Once this happened, my life became a mess and I was very busy, trying to catch up for the two years I'd missed. And then, as my life became more complicated, I didn't pay as strict attention to answering letters as perhaps I should have. Time passed more quickly than I could have ever imagined and suddenly, it's fifty years later.

As I sit here, trying to figure out what I should say to you, I can't help but wonder how things would have turned out if only I could have thrown a ball as fast as the years have passed. If I'd only been a little better, just a little stronger, I might have actually risen to the level of mediocrity, perhaps even been good enough for a college team somewhere. Of course, I'll never know, but I suspect I'd have had enough sense to realize I only had a modest talent, and it was foolish to pursue a dream that required so much more talent than I ever had.

But I also know you're not interested in this kind of thing; you want to know what I think about your article in The Sporting News, and, as you requested, I obtained a copy of the article. Literally a copy, since it was no longer easy to obtain an original, certainly not by sending in stamps and requesting a back issue. Maybe an original copy will turn up, but for the time being I'll be content to just have the words. It turned out a friend, Nick Niles, was the publisher of this fine publication for a few years, and he asked someone to dig into the archives, and retrieve the words you wrote half a century ago.

I read your article carefully, thought about it for some while and have come to some conclusions about the incident it describes. It's been nearly one hundred years since that game in Detroit, but generally, things aren't so different in 2oo5 than they were in 19o9. The only difference is that sporting events are often much more extreme these days, have larger audiences, generate much more media coverage and are driven by commercial considerations that would astound the most avaricious club owner in 19o9. And by extreme, I mean extreme. There is now something called "extreme sports," where people court danger, sometimes for money, sometimes not, life and death danger and in many other instances athletes actually try to maim their opponents. Overt violence is commonplace; some teams regularly employ bruisers who's only talent is to break fingers in football pileup, crush skulls with a hockey stick, or cause other kinds of bodily harm.

I hope you don't find this offensive, but you want to know what I think and this is the best I can come up with. I feel you were undoubtedly a rough and tumble guy, a man with serious psychological damage, a large ego and probably a persecution complex. Yet you also had extraordinary athletic ability and perhaps equally important, were highly intelligent. Your own psyche may have been damaged, but this didn't keep you from being a profoundly psychological ballplayer, maybe the first who used it so profoundly.

I suspect you used your terrible reputation to great advantage. Who knows if you sat in the dugout and filed your spikes razor sharp, but if your opponents thought you did, it gave you a competitive edge. As I said, you were one of the first baseball players to use your mind to take care of the opposition.

The so-called "Baker spiking" may well be a case in point. You may have managed to beat the tag because Baker feared your flying feet. I read your explanation of the incident and I've looked at the photograph for over fifty years. It seems to make sense to me. The incident took place in 1909, and in retrospect, the historical aspect is interesting.

I looked up Frank "Home Run" Baker's playing statistics for that year. He played in 148 of Philadelphia's 153 games; he also led the league in triples. Your claim that if you'd hurt Baker so bad, why didn't he miss any games, why did he play in their next series. Good points, I think.

In checking Baker's statistics, I came upon something else. In that year he was just plain old Frank Baker, the "Home Run" came later. Who, I wondered, led the league in home runs that year? A quick check revealed it was you, and then I noticed something else. In 1909 you not only led the American League, but the National League as well in batting average, total bases, hits, slugging percentage, runs batted in, home runs, home run percentage and stolen bases. You also led the American League in runs scored. You had led your own league in nine categories and both leagues in eight!

You may have been a terror on the base paths and personally very unpleasant, but it also seems you were probably so much better than anyone else playing at the time, that you outplayed and outwitted so many of your opponents, that a wee bit of envy might be behind much of the mudslinging. You were also probably horrible to the guys who followed baseball for the papers, so they wrote about you in a disparaging way.

Did you ever have a run-in with Horace Fogel, or was he just a guy trying to cause trouble? Then as now, if someone can stir up trouble by saying you did this or that, it sold papers, just like the supermarket rags do today. Except today they sell more copies and television can spread the word even more effectively. Or was he just a disgruntled guy, who'd once been very active in baseball and was now reduced to just writing about it?

An additional factor is probably your not inconsequential ego. Think about how baseball players react to publicity, favorable and unfavorable in 2oo5. If a player comes in first in a couple of categories, he's put on a pedestal. I wonder how the media would treat somebody today who won virtually every offensive category possible? My guess is the writers and nightly news sport personalities would treat such a player like the Second Coming, even if he bit the heads off chickens in the outfield. No one resorted to things like that in your day, nor did they have to, but even though you won everything there was to win, you were vilified and this bothered you. Again, I hope this doesn't offend you, but it seems to me you were just an extraordinarily talented, but socially maladjusted man, crying out for respect.

I read somewhere that you were the dirtiest player who ever lived, but the only place you had any opportunity to be "dirty" was while running bases, and you freely admit to nailing a couple of pitchers who tried to bean you. I suspect you probably tore into a few more, but it is charming that after nearly half a century, you still will not name the two offending pitchers. You were an outfielder, so you had few opportunities to throw a ball at anyone from the field. As far as I know, no one ever accused you of hitting the catcher with your bat (as I once saw a modern player do) and as far as I know you were in sufficient control of your bat, that you didn't regularly throw it into the stands, as some players do today.

Any number of players today are praised for being supreme competitors. My guess is that you exceeded the norms of respectful competition of the day, and used his athletic prowess and decidedly superior intellect to crush and humiliate your opponents. This did not engender much love for you on the part of your peers or the fans, except in Detroit, but the public's hatred probably just drove you all the harder.

On a personal level, there is an obvious question. If you were such a terrible person, why were you so kind to me? I know you can't answer this right now, but were you searching for respect anywhere you could find it, even the respect of an unknown kid three thousand miles away? If you were really a totally unrepentant scoundrel, a man with no socially redeeming features, wouldn't you have flung my innocent letter into the nearest garbage can? After all, as you pointed out in one letter to me, I hadn't bothered to include postage and an envelope for your reply, and in another you said you didn't throw it in the wastebasket because it made sense.

Yet, you were not only polite in answering my letter and signing the bits of memorabilia, but you invested three cents in the process. Perhaps the answer to your puzzling behavior may be as simple as what the saxophonist Zoot Sims once said to me, about his some-time associate, Stan Getz. When I asked what he thought about Getz, who was charming one moment and horrid the next, Sims replied, He's an interesting bunch of guys. There were probably many layers to your personality, some were undoubtedly very unpleasant, but others may have been charming. Maybe I was lucky to have caught you on four or five good days and have the letters and memories to prove it. But the odds against just catching you on good days seem pretty slim.

A wise old poet from Wales, also known to have an extra
personality or two, once said on a BBC broadcast in the
early 1950's, The memories of childhood have no order
and no end and this is precisely the point of my
thoughts about my letters from you and the other ball
players who wrote to me or autographed and returned
the little scraps of paper, pictures clipped from
magazines or bubble gum cards.

It's true, there's no order to the memories I have of you
and those other players, and I've surely messed up the
truth somewhere in my remembrances, but I know all
those scraps of paper meant a lot to me when I
desperately needed them. You sent me more wonderful
pictures, autographs and letters than anyone, and they
really made a difference to me, and they still do. And
if it makes any difference, I believe your explanation
of the so-called "spiking."

More importantly, I believe that the game you and your
teammates and opponents played all those years ago was
a little cleaner than it is today. You may have
occasionally spiked someone sliding into second, but
you didn't regularly spike your system with drugs,
other than possibly cigarettes. You didn't need agents
and while you wanted to make a buck, you didn't just
play for the money. You didn't start brawls for the sake
of ticket sales and the best pitcher of your era, Walter
Johnson, never threw at anyone's head, because he knew
he could hit it and it would kill him dead. And no one
sat behind a table selling autographs to wide-eyed kids
standing in line. You may have been a horror to your
opponents on the field and uncivil to your many
enemies, but I'll bet you never charged a kid for an
autograph.

I'm sorry I've gone on so long, but I've had fifty years
to think about some of these things and, unfortunately,
I'm taking them out on you. It's been quite a few years

since you made your request, and I don't know if you
ever received the respect you felt you deserved, but in
2oo5 you're doing just fine in the respect department.
You were the subject of a Hollywood movie, books and
articles continue to flood the market, and you are
inching towards a million entries on most Internet
search engines. You probably don't know what that
means, but it's a good thing and the entries are mostly
all positive. On the other hand, there are a few entries
for Horace Fogel, but not many. Thanks for fifty years
of good memories.

Sincerely,

Hank O'Neal

ACKNOWLEDGMENTS

I don't remember exactly when I wrote the handful of words that began the nearly thirty-year journey that has ended with the publication of *Sincerely, Ty Cobb* in 2020, but I do remember those first words, at least those that make up the first sentence. The first sentence in 1990 or 1991 is the same published here, in 2020: *I often wonder why I remember so much about playing baseball when I was a kid growing up in Fort Worth.* But one thing that is very clear is because it has been a nearly thirty years from those first words until today, many people have helped me along the way to bring this slim volume to fruition.

In the early 1990s, when I first began work on this book, there were a handful of people who were encouraging. Jacqueline Onassis and Margaret Whitton have been mentioned, but Paul Bacon, who designed the cover, has not, and Nick Niles who found and had the rights to an important Ty Cobb article also made a major contribution.

Paul was an important, maybe the most important, US-based book jacket designer of the last seventy years, and proved it by designing over 6500 dust jackets. Three of the more well known are *Catch-22*, *One Flew Over the Cuckoo's Nest,* and *Portnoy's Complaint.* He also did three for me that are not so well known. Nick was and is an old friend. In the early 1990s and beyond, Nick was the president of Sporting News Publishing. He not only found the Ty Cobb article but gave me permission to use it. And not to be overlooked, Shelley Shier, my partner in various activities then as now, didn't complain too much when I spent time working on the book, even though she and I were both aware this was taking my time and energy away from more profitable endeavors.

In between the early 1990s and 2018, when Dan Williams, the director of TCU Press, expressed an interest in it, *Sincerely, Ty Cobb* languished, as I worked on other books and attended to other matters. All that was accomplished to move this project forward was that all the illustrations included in the book were carefully scanned, and high-resolution files were saved and in some cases enhanced if the source material contained any imperfections. Ian P. Clifford scanned all the illustrations, made the fixes, and created the files used to create the book. Without these perfectly rendered images there would be no book.

But even though TCU was interested in publishing the book there was another hurdle to overcome. Some of the material I wanted to use as illustrations were old baseball cards from the late 1940s and early 1950s, and even though some legal authorities felt that fair use rules might apply to them it was felt it would be best to secure permission from The Topps Company for their use, since the majority of the cards were issued by that company.

I discovered that Michael Eisner owned The Topps Company. I wrote a letter to Mr. Eisner which I passed along to Warren Spector (Margaret Whitton's husband), who in turn made sure the letter reached Michael Eisner. Permission to use the cards was granted a few days later in the form of a letter from Valerie Fabbro, the Topp's associate general counsel. I'm sure there were others at Topps who helped with this, but I am unaware of their names.

Once the permissions hurdle was cleared, Dan Williams's TCU team took over. Kathy Walton and Molly Spain skillfully edited and fixed up my almost thirty-year-old wandering prose; Preston Thomas created an imaginative layout; Melinda Esco shepherded the book through the various phases of production; and Rebecca Allen made sure the book had an internet presence about six months before it was scheduled to be published, just to make sure all of Ty Cobb's many fans were aware a book was on the way.

Thanks are offered to all these extraordinary people who helped make *Sincerely, Ty Cobb* possible.

APPENDIX
TRANSCRIPTIONS OF
TY COBB LETTERS

The First Letter from Hank to Ty Cobb and Cobb's Response

Dear Mr. Cobb,

You have always been one of my favorite ballplayers, as, my grandfather played with you. His name was Curtis Austin Christian, he did not play with you in the majors, only in Macon, Georgia, where he lived. He was a pitcher and his picture was in the "Life" magazine in the article you wrote. It was a picture of the sandlot team you were on in Georgia.

I read every word in that series of "Life" magazine articles, and since I was only 12 it was something. I really got a lot out of it, I guess the main thing was hitting to all fields. It really helped me, now I can do it easily. If I could pick it up I don't see why Ted Williams and some of the others couldn't. Because of hitting to all fields I have yet to be put out playing ball in gym, 7 for 7, 6 singles and 1 double, but I can't get much power unless I just stand and hit away. I agreed with most of the things in your article in "Life." I don't guess you mentioned Rosen or Kluszewski because they had not quite hit there prime. I don't think that you gave "Pee Wee" Reese enough credit, as he has held up pretty well. I think you should have mentioned Bob Feller more, as I think he is the best pitcher that has come along in quite a while, if he hadn't gone to war he would be close to 400 wins instead of 300.

I wrote to you about six months ago, in Detroit, but it was the wrong Ty Cobb. He wrote me a letter telling me he sent it to you but I guess it got lost.

I would like to know who your favorite pitcher to hit was, I guess you did equally great against all of them, but who was your favorite to hit and who was your worst pitcher to hit?

I am enclosing two pictures and a piece of paper I wish you would autograph and return. Your fan, Harold L. O'Neal, Jr. 14/2/55

Dear Harold:

I note the fault you found in my life stories, not mentioning certain players. I had only 12,000 words allotted to me to use, the subject was selected or given to me by "Life" I did not choose. If you were a <u>very</u> <u>careful</u> reader of the story before you formed and expressed an opinion, you would have seen & realized – <u>I</u> <u>said</u> Musial & <u>Rizzuto</u> <u>was</u> <u>type</u> <u>and</u> <u>example</u> of both players of moderns who could have played on old timer teams. I had to use only 12,000 words. Of course Reese & many others yes Feller is a real or was a fine pitcher not because he is your favorite, he with any other modern pitcher cannot be placed on an all time pitching staff. You have to go to the old-timers, see <u>records</u>, that counts – how could you place any modern pitcher on all time – Johnson, Mathewson, Alexander, Walsh, Plank, Grove, old Cy Young <u>many</u> <u>others</u>. Let's be right in all this. <u>RECORDS</u>

You have to be <u>right</u> as I was, should have enclosed for convenience an addressed and stamped envelope – I receive an average of 4 requests for autographs alone.

THE SECOND LETTER
FROM TY COBB

Menlo Park, Calif. 3/14/55

Dear Harold Neal:-

Yours received, my letter was more to explain, not that I thought you were criticizing. I do receive many letters from people who write and in some they differ or criticize also so very few or possibly all are ignorant of the subject, there is only one way, that is what are facts and truth. (I am not referring to you) the <u>records</u> are available, yet they don't go to the trouble of getting them and being sure to be right. You seem to like baseball I am going to trouble to write you and give title of a book, rather small, pocket size that have a greater part of all players records, and in any difference of opinions a person with this book can win such arguments also I find this book and records so very interesting myself and many of the players I ~~plaid~~ played with or against for many years, and yet I have more books of records, yearly records all leagues, books written that you might have trouble jumping over and yet I find this book my favorite and so easy to refer to. You write to Mr. Johnson Spink, 2018 Washington Ave., St. Louis, (3) Mo. (that's the Sporting News) ask him price on "Daguerreo Types" of great baseball Stars. Get you one of these and you will thank me.

You ask me of the book "Busting EM" I have it saw it the other day in cleaning out and arranging books etc. I have looked for it and cannot locate it, I have far too many of all kinds of books. You mention of it being written or printed 1914 well that's too far back to be complete as I played until 1928.

Now there are many baseball books written also quite a few thats a disagree and not worth the paper and by so-called writers that are not recognized by the sports writers. These fellows gather up old fake stories, print them in books and add provocative stories of their own, at the expense of the player who is a star or records of such – a name – they never right of John Smith, Brown or Jones and the story has to be critical and where the name player is shown up, there has been so many stories printed absolutely a lie and never happened but many read and believe them, these stories are put in books to cause them to sell. Ted Williams today is an example of mistreatment. A creature Gene Schor* by name wrote a book and it was gotten out hurriedly to capitalize on all the interest caused by the Life stories I did. This book is scandalous also I have never met or remember seeing Schor even. He had Atlanta Georgia newspaperman Bishler** to do so called research in the section I lived. I knew Bishler and after Schor's book I had a friend go to Bishler and asked if he was responsible for things of Ga. about me, in book, Bishlers answer was unprintable, he cursed Schor, saying he went to expense of auto travel and lots of time in my section, submitted his work which he was to be paid for. Schor ~~he~~ did not use most of it, ~~I~~ never paid him a dime, but used Bishlers name in expressing appreciation which was for only one reason to add the dignity of Bishlers name. Mind you I did not go to Bishler not that he would lie to me, but I to make sure, had a friend of mine also of Bishlers go to him.

Schor is one man I would have taken to court, even conferred with a lawyer but remember anyone can write a book or story and if they say for instance, The Story of Ty Cobb (big letters) and then use very small "by" Gene Schoor, if Schor is a bum and has nothing, one cannot do anything except publicity which draws public's attention and curiosity also increase sales of book. So if you want legitimate books of baseball then select a legitimate writer anyone else watch out for that word "by." Get the book I advised then compare older players with modern's records yourself.

Sincerely,
Ty Cobb

P.S. You can write me but I can't answer any more -

*Eugene R. Schoor
** Furman Bishler, the *Atlanta Journal-Constitution*

THE THIRD LETTER
FROM TY COBB

Tyrus R. Cobb
48 Spencer Lane, Atherton
Menlo Park, California
4/15/55

Dear Harold O'Neal, Jr: -

No one as in your case could be blamed for thinking your carefully and thoughtfully prepared communication intended for me had been lost or possibly ignored as much time have elapsed since you address yours to the wrong Ty Cobb, though you were informed by the Ty Cobb in Detroit (now) that in his kindness advised you, he had forwarded yours on to me, this he informed me by letter last November, so you have a right to feel obligated to Mr. Cobb, Audet? Detroit or Dearborn Michigan as he did his part at once. I was away in the east for 6 weeks and as usual confronted with a lot of mail, requests for autographs and advice on baseball etc. This constitutes quite a task for me coupled with other duties of mine so time has passed, but in time I respond or try to and as you see I have finally gotten to yours. I always feel honored and complimented with such requests, though am forced to say, with the task, I sometimes wish the demands would lessen. I am returning as you see your pictures autographed also another one I add one reason for this is that so many make <u>demands</u> and then never have the consideration ~~to~~ they should and also their duty to do, in sending the ~~matt~~ material then the request and take care of return address, stamps etc. So I commend you my boy doing this, his material and request will never reach the waste paper basket. I apologize for my delay as I explained above. I am,

Sincerely,
Ty Cobb

P.S. Your mention of autographing pictures and <u>the</u> <u>piece</u> <u>of</u> <u>paper</u>, the paper must have gotten misplaced here, I enclose another of mine.
Ty

THE FOURTH LETTER FROM TY COBB

Tyrus R Cobb

Harold:-

The picture I send is of the so called Baker spiking which I was so unfairly accused of by a drunken sports writer Horace Fogel* of some Phila. paper this play was in Detroit so he writes a lurid story really to arouse the fans in Phila so when Detroit came there next, would boost the attendance—this has been a practice by the unscrupulous writers. I have always resented this deeply in the play happened in 1909—46 years ago and is still referred to, now very few not more than six people have a reprint of this play, so you are one of them. I am sending a request of you, if you cannot get the March 2nd 1955 edition of Sporting News (baseball) 2018 Washington Ave, St. Louis (3) Mo. I request you write them send return postage and the cost of paper in stamps, 25 cents tell them why you want it to read Cobbs explanation of Baker spiking, you will no doubt have your stamps returned and will receive this edition, do not mention I asked you to do this. You will understand it all then, also with the picture I send you, will have an unusual souvenir, I think: Write me when and if you do this, also your opinion.

—Ty—
*Horace Solomon Fogel

ABOUT THE AUTHOR

Photo by Arthur Elgort

HANK O'NEAL was born in Kilgore, Texas, in 1940. His career has included the world of government, education, music, photography, and literature.

O'Neal was employed by the Central Intelligence Agency from 1963 until he "retired" in 1976 and began the next phase of his life. He had heard his first jazz records when he was a teenager. He liked what he heard and kept on listening. In the sixty-five years since that first awakening, he has formed two record companies (Chiaroscuro and Hammond Music Enterprises); built two recording studios; produced over 200 jazz LPs/CDs and 100 music festivals (The Floating Jazz Festival, The Blues Cruise et al); published a number of books and articles on jazz; photographed most of the giants of jazz from the second half of the twentieth century; exhibited these photographs regularly; and joined and continues to serve on the boards of various nonprofit organizations that serve the jazz community, including the Jazz and Contemporary Music Program of the New School (1985), The Jazz Foundation of America (1993), The Jazz Gallery (1996), and more recently The National Jazz Museum in Harlem (2008 - 2012). He continues to serve as an advisor to the Oslo Jazz Festival (1986), the Bern Jazz Festival (2005), and George Wein's New Festival Productions (2007). In 2018 all these activities continue unabated.

In 1970, O'Neal took what he considers his first serious photographs and in 1972 met Berenice Abbott, with whom he worked closely for nineteen years. About the same time, he met André Kertèsz, Walker Evans, and all the other living FSA photographers and many other exceptional photographic artists who were all to influence him. His own photographs have been widely exhibited and reproduced since that time. O'Neal published his first book in 1973, but his first to gain widespread attention was *A Vision Shared* (1976). Steidl reissued this important book in 2018. He has published over twenty books on other subjects, mostly related to photography, his own or others, music, or both. In addition to *A Vision Shared*, Steidl will release four other new books by O'Neal, *You've Got to Do a Damn Sight Better than That, Buster* (2020), a memoir of his experiences working with Abbott for nineteen years; *Berenice Abbott's Maine – The Color Photographs, Maine 1960s – 1970s* (with Berenice Abbott); and *Berenice Abbott: In Her Own Words.* He was recently coeditor of the five volumes included in *The Unknown Abbott* (Steidl, 2013) and *Berenice Abbott – The Paris Portraits* (Steidl, 2015). His most recent publication is *Preserving Lives* (TCU Press, 2018).

Since his retrospective at New York City's legendary Witkin Gallery in 1999 he has had dozens of exhibitions in both museums and commercial galleries. He is particularly proud of his three exhibitions in East Texas at the Longview Museum of Fine Arts that began in 2006. He is currently working on a project featuring forty-five years of his work in East Texas along US Highway 80 and a series of books related to documenting street art in New York City. He currently resides in New York City.